THE C

NELSON CABRAL

M000195391

PRAISE FOR NELSON CABRAL AND
THE CREATIVE STORM

"*The Creative Storm* gives business leaders and managers in any industry an actionable plan to implement creativity throughout all levels of their organization. Author Nelson Cabral distills an imaginative framework for boosting any business by igniting a *Creative Storm* in innovation and competitiveness through a series of simple, yet effective steps."

— **DAVID BOSSERT**, PRODUCER, CREATIVE DIRECTOR & HEAD OF SPECIAL PROJECTS, THE WALT DISNEY COMPANY

"Fan-flipping-tastic!"

— **DAVID NEWMAN**, CSP, AUTHOR OF "DO IT! MARKETING"

"LOVE *THE CREATIVE STORM* SO MUCH! If you've ever suspected your company could be on the verge of something great, *The Creative Storm* offers an effective and comprehensive road map to make it happen. Creativity is innovation's rocket fuel. Using Cabral's methodology, leaders can create an invested culture where the latent talent throughout their organization can be unleashed. I especially like Nelson's ideas around fearless leadership and investing in every employee, at every level, to have a safe space for creativity. If the status quo is your kryptonite, you'll love this book."

— **ALLISON DICK**, DIRECTOR, DIGITAL CONTENT - MARKETING SOLUTIONS & CUSTOMER EXPERIENCE (CX), XEROX / FORMER CONTENT STRATEGIST, CORUS ENTERTAINMENT

"Nelson rocks!"

— **CHAD SMITH**, RED HOT CHILI PEPPERS, INDUCTEE, THE ROCK AND ROLL HALL OF FAME

"It was truly delightful to see Nelson and *The Creative Storm* in action and keynoting in London at our European Lotteries / World Lottery Association Marketing Summit. One rarely sees such dedication and passion in a speaker tailor-making a presentation for a specific audience. His performance and training for our participants was outstanding, both in content and delivery. Bravo!"

— **ANDRÉ NOËL CHAKER**, CURATOR & MODERATOR, WORLD LOTTERY ASSOCIATION / EUROPEAN LOTTERIES EVENT DIRECTOR / OWNER, C&C GLOBAL ADVOCATES OY

"Highly creative! Nelson knocked it out of the park for us."

— **MARIA VISOCCHI**, DIRECTOR OF MARKETING, ADIDAS

"If you need help in creating synergy and elevating performance in your organization, we recommend Nelson and *The Creative Storm*. We loved him because of his contagious enthusiasm and willingness to genuinely listen to our management team and employees. The outcome of Nelson's work was our leaders being prepared to drive innovation and business growth, capture employee commitment and elevate productivity and performance."

— **ANDREW PETERS**, PARTNER / GENERAL MANAGER, MERCEDES-BENZ

"Nelson's *Creative Storm* Keynote and Full-Day Workshop at our National Project Management Symposium was fantastic! I thoroughly enjoyed it and it gave me and our leadership and project management audience the Creative Leadership boost we were looking for!"

— **SHANNON MCLELLAN**, SENIOR CONFERENCE DIRECTOR, NATIONAL CAPITAL PROJECT MANAGEMENT SYMPOSIUM / PROJECT MANAGEMENT INSTITUTE

"Nelson has the uncanny ability to walk into any room, bring people together and inspire them to create truly amazing results."

— **MIGUEL LEBLANC**, COMMUNICATIONS COORDINATOR, COMMUNICATIONS AND MARKETING BRANCH, INNOVATION, SCIENCE AND ECONOMIC DEVELOPMENT CANADA / GOVERNMENT OF CANADA

"Nelson is the next Woody Allen or Mike Clattenburg. He truly understands how to inspire and guide highly creative and artistic individuals and teams—and lead them to high standards of performance. To thrive as a leader in innovative, artistic, entrepreneurial environments, you must allow the freedom to take risks and not inhibit the creative process, but ignite it. Nelson gets that, and knows how to find that balance. It was amazing to see him in action and learn from him. Every leader of a creative company should!"

— **BERNARD ROBICHAUD**, PRODUCER / AWARD-WINNING ACTOR, TRAILER PARK BOYS / NETFLIX

"I was at a leadership conference where the Keynote Speaker was Nelson Cabral who made a really great presentation on innovation and Creative Leadership. The perspective that caught my attention was that while many speak to what innovation is, and how to innovate, he spoke to The 9 Forces of Creative Leadership that can help leaders to unleash *The Creative Storm* in their organization. Nelson's experience and extremely engaging personality, as well as his passion for helping leaders to help themselves, would, in my opinion, help any organization get enthused and excited about innovation and creativity. I would strongly recommend that you consider him as a suitable speaker at any event or executive learning opportunity."

— **SHERIN V EMMANUEL MIS**, PMP, INFORMATION ARCHITECT, INFORMATION MANAGEMENT DIVISION, CANADA REVENUE AGENCY

"I admit the honor of hosting Mr. Cabral at our offices in Warsaw, Poland, where he enraptured the staff and management with his winning formula for unlocking the hidden creative treasures within."

— **JOHN VAN KANNEL**, CEO / MANAGING DIRECTOR, THE LOWE GROUP, WARSAW, POLAND (LOWE GGK, PANMEDIA WESTERN, GGK PR)

"*The Creative Storm* was an amazing keynote by Nelson at our Global POLARIS Forum in Riga, Latvia. An outstanding case study and great inspiration to be innovative and a Creative Leader. Thank you for those very practical tips to boost creativity at any organization!"

— **AGNESE ZAGATA**, BUSINESS CONFERENCE ORGANIZER, GLOBAL POLARIS SUMMIT, INVESTMENT AND DEVELOPMENT AGENCY OF LATVIA

"Nelson's Opening *Creative Storm* keynote presentation to our Project Managers at our North American Conference was highly engaging and he was able to convey A LOT of useful management skills and strategies. Here's what I heard from some of our PMIers / audience members: 'Loved the "Lord Nelson" approach to be innovative—I will use it for my business; Great pace and masterful delivery; Nelson was great, and I'd love to see keynote speakers like him for our global events; Nelson was an outstanding presenter and gave our team and managers a much needed spark and boost.'"

— MICHAEL G. SMITH PMP, REGION 3 SUMMIT CONFERENCE DIRECTOR / PROJECT MANAGER, PROJECT MANAGEMENT INSTITUTE

"Nelson is highly creative in bringing new and never-before-seen management team development experiences and corporate training to our Executive Team."

— LUANNE ZHU, CUSTOMER EXPERIENCE STRATEGY MANAGER, MERCEDES-BENZ CANADA, TORONTO CORPORATE HEAD OFFICE

"Beneath Nelson's warm and friendly demeanor exists a refined, powerful and visionary Creative Director. The value of what Nelson does goes beyond his creativity—it is also passion and accountability that drives his desire to service clients and grow their business."

— ROBERT STOKES, DIRECTOR, STRATEGY & PLANNING / VICE PRESIDENT, SOCIAL RESPONSIBILITY AND COMMUNICATIONS, ATLANTIC LOTTERY CORPORATION

"Imaginative and highly creative. An enthusiastic, seasoned Innovation Director with impressive innovation capabilities. Very capable of addressing business strategy in a dynamic, appealing manner. Infectious, positive energy. Nelson is an engaging presenter and has a talent for simplifying business challenges into compelling ideas and solutions. Thoroughly enjoyed working with Nelson."
— **SUE BULMER**, MANAGER, COMMUNICATIONS, BELL

"I have had the pleasure of seeing two versions of Nelson's *Creative Storm* LIVE Innovation Management & Culture Change Program. I have thoroughly enjoyed it and highly recommend it to everyone. Regardless of the nature of your business or activity, creativity can help you move forward and Nelson can show you how. His many real-life examples clearly demonstrate that he has learned world-class innovation management from real experience. Thank you Nelson, for sharing *The Creative Storm* and your inspirational ideas on the art of leading innovation."
— **DARREN BROWN**, VP SERVICE DELIVERY, PROJECT MANAGEMENT INSTITUTE / CGI GROUP INC., SENIOR IT PROJECT MANAGER AND BUSINESS ANALYST

"Loved Nelson's *Creative Storm* Program! Gained new tools and strategies for igniting a more innovative culture. A great complement and supplement to how I'm leading and managing my teams."
— **PNINA MINTZ**, PH.D., CHIEF CULTURE OFFICER, EXECUTIVE VICE PRESIDENT, CENTER FOR NEUROLOGICAL AND NEURODEVELOPMENTAL HEALTH / BOARD MEMBER, NEW JERSEY MEDICAL GROUP MANAGEMENT ASSOCIATION

"Nelson's full day seminar to our agency management and team was practical, insightful and energizing. Amazing!"
— **BARTEK BARTOSZEK**, OWNER AND CREATIVE DIRECTOR, TBWA WARSAW

"Articulate. Persuasive. Energetic. Nelson has a genuine interest in helping leaders and teams solve marketing, advertising and innovation problems."
— **MARTIN SHEWCHUK**, VP, CHIEF CREATIVE OFFICER, LEO BURNETT

"With 'fear of the new' a barrier for us, and our team going through a culture rebuilding initiative, Nelson's Creative Leadership Force 4 'Activate Climates' is a game-changer for me. If you want to ignite your healthcare culture and team to innovate better together and drive change, *The Creative Storm* is the solution."
— **VALERIE MARTINET**, BOARD MEMBER, CALIFORNIA MEDICAL GROUP MANAGEMENT ASSOCIATION / DISTRICT SALES AGENT, SENIOR REPRESENTATIVE, AUTHORIZED INDEPENDENT CONTRACTOR OF TRANSWORLD SYSTEMS INC. (TSI)

"Nelson's *Creative Storm* is amazing and took us to the next level of creativity and innovation. His process helped 'turn over some stones' to start the conversation on creativity within our organization. We were also trying to tackle the 'capacity' issue that all our leaders are struggling with, that inevitably, is not going away anytime soon within our organization. I have heard some really positive feedback from our teams and posted Nelson's '10 Ways to Become an Easy Collaborator' Poster and the 3 "Nelson Touch" Levels in our offices to get people to see them often."
— **LCOL ANGIE LAPOINTE**, CD COS DCSEM, ADM(MAT) DGLEPM, CANADIAN ARMED FORCES

"Nelson's game-changing Innovation Consulting has reinvented our potential. He helped us come up with a radical new value proposition, empowered us to identify unexpected opportunities, create disruptive ideas, rethink our customers and differentiate our brand."

— **TERI MALTAIS**, SVP MARKETING, RTTECH SOFTWARE

"When Nelson first showed up, our management and teams all thought we would be getting yet another run of the mill keynote speaker and corporate trainer. But that is not what we got. Nelson's *Creative Storm* delivered the most engaging and interactive presentation that our company has ever had. Nelson's deep knowledge about his subject, and his ability to present in a highly engaging and impactful way completely inspired my team to return to work excited to reach new levels of creativity and innovation."

— **GREG HEMMINGS**, CEO / EXECUTIVE PRODUCER,
HEMMINGS HOUSE PICTURES

"Nelson's business keynotes and innovation consulting are thoughtful and engaging. He analyzed the issues our team was having and presented actionable tools and strategies. I was particularly impressed with his interaction with employees, always putting them at ease and encouraging them to speak freely throughout his program."

— **GREG CHRISANTHIDIS**, CUSTOMER EXPERIENCE MANAGER,
MERCEDES-BENZ CANADA, TORONTO CORPORATE HEAD OFFICE

"Nelson entertained and inspired our students with his stellar *Creative Storm* presentation again this year. His depth of knowledge and experience shows his real creative genius."
— **DALE RITCHIE**, PRESIDENT, MCKENZIE COLLEGE
SCHOOL OF ART AND DESIGN

"Nelson brought his *Creative Storm* to our annual executive three-day retreat. With some recent challenges with the Executive Team, Nelson's program was an excellent way to boost morale and productivity, while squeezing in some excellent leadership, teamwork and communications skills development. Because of Nelson, this was our BEST executive retreat ever! A Speaking Program from Nelson will energize your team to take on the world!"
— **BRUCE FITCH**, MINISTER OF JUSTICE & CONSUMER AFFAIRS, MINISTER
OF ECONOMIC DEVELOPMENT, GOVERNMENT OF NEW BRUNSWICK

"In my seven years working with Nelson, I experienced a results-oriented individual with superior leadership skills, while retaining the ability to be a team player. I regard him as a reliable and trustworthy management consultant with an excellent record of guiding and advising on high level management issues. If you are a C-level leader who needs help accelerating innovation and change, I have no hesitation whatsoever in recommending Nelson."
— **HAZEL MCCALLION**, MAYOR OF MISSISSAUGA, ORDER OF CANADA IN
2005, RUNNER-UP IN WORLD MAYOR 2005,
LONGEST SERVING MAYOR IN CANADA

"Nelson is a multi-talented, highly intelligent Innovation Director and Keynote Speaker at the top of the North American market. He has the unique talent of understanding business analysis, priorities and imperatives; and uncovering strategies that meet the challenge. A true renaissance individual, he knows how to push the creative envelope while facilitating and presenting highly effective, real-world business strategies and results."
— **DAVID A. MCALLISTER**, VICE PRESIDENT, JAM INDUSTRIES LTD.

"I just want to congratulate you for a fabulous *Creative Storm* presentation. It is unusual for a presenter to frame the issues so precisely, getting just the right mix of big-picture objectives and rubber-hits-road specificity about what to do about it. Frankly, most keynote speakers do okay on the big-picture inspiration angle, or if they come from an operational role they do well on the details of execution. It's just that few can do both, and it is so vital to do both for the presentation to connect with the audience and have relevant impact. Thank you for connecting all the dots. I accepted *The Creative Storm Challenge* and have already embarked on new ways to reinvent our business!"
— **PAUL JASON**, CEO, PUBLIC GAMING RESEARCH INSTITUTE / EDITOR, EUROPEAN LOTTERIES NEWS MAGAZINE

"Nelson's annual multi-day retreats and executive team development workshops held every year are challenging, motivating and inspiring. Love his 'Roxercises'. Our senior team always returns from them enlightened and reinvigorated to ignite innovation in our business, culture and brands. Even better, Nelson has the ability to help us translate inspiration into action."

— JIM ROCKWELL, VICE PRESIDENT, DIRECTOR OF MARKETING, LATIN PERCUSSION HEADQUARTERS, GARFIELD, NEW JERSEY, USA

"Nelson's training and facilitating was absolutely perfect for our executive team and employees. I was getting overwhelmed with what seemed like so many things to fix. But with his Two-Day Program, Nelson really brought clarity to what needed to be worked on. And better yet, simplified it for me. I must say, Nelson is an excellent listener. I find that a rare treat nowadays. The staff and Executive Team REALLY enjoyed it and he made a huge impact on our organization."

— KEN ROBINSON, FIXED OPERATION MANAGER, MERCEDES-BENZ

"We've held many strategic work sessions, corporate team-building executive meetings, and staff training seminars facilitated and led by Nelson. We look forward to these meetings because they were creative and different each time and always resulted in new ideas that we were able to develop into our corporate culture, business strategies and brands."

— HEIDI SCHAEFFER, EXECUTIVE CREATIVE DIRECTOR, KAMAN MUSIC CORPORATION, GLOBAL HEADQUARTERS, BLOOMFIELD, CONNECTICUT, USA

"Nelson's drive to help us succeed could be felt in every executive presentation he made and every corporate meeting he facilitated. His Creative Leadership and inspiration has resulted in the most innovative and successful campaigns in our company's history. He brings an easy collaboration to his client relationships, with an open mindedness that seeks to simplify business challenges into compelling ideas. Nelson also brings a sense of entrepreneurial spirit to each initiative and believes strongly that SABIAN's success was his success."

— **STACEY MONTGOMERY-CLARK**, VP OF MARKETING, SABIAN CYMBALS LTD.

THE CREATIVE LEADERSHIP MANIFESTO

THE CREATIVE STORM

UNLEASHING THE 9 FORCES
OF CREATIVE LEADERSHIP

NELSON CABRAL

THE WORLD'S ONLY TRIPLE THREAT
CREATIVE LEADERSHIP EXPERT

Copyright © CABRAL Creative Leadership International Inc., 2018

All Rights Reserved.

Without limiting the rights under copyright reserved above, no part of this publication may be reproduced, stored in or introduced into a retrieval system, or transmitted, in any form or by any means (electronic, mechanical, photocopying, recording or otherwise), without the prior written permission of both the copyright owner and the above publisher of this book.

The scanning, uploading and distribution of this book via the internet or via any other means without the permission of the publisher is illegal and punishable by law. Please purchase only authorized printed or electronic editions and do not participate in or encourage electronic piracy of copyrighted materials. Your support of the author's rights is appreciated.

ISBN 978-1-9994069-0-5 (pbk.)
ISBN 978-1-9994069-1-2 (ebk)

Edited by Christopher Murray
Cover Design by James Wheldon
Text Design & Layout by Linda Parke (www.ravenbookdesign.com)

Printed and bound in Canada by Friesens

To Mom and Dad . . .
who gave me the freedom to unleash *Creative Storms*.

To Gary . . .
who reminded me I was "*The Creative Storm.*"

To Karen, Jasmine, Finnian and Mira . . .
you continually inspire me to be a better
Creative Leader and role model.
I love you.

BECAUSE OF THE
DIGITAL TRANSFORMATION,
CREATIVE LEADERSHIP
IS NOW THE MOST
IN-DEMAND LEADERSHIP
STYLE IN ALL INDUSTRIES.

THE CREATIVE STORM

noun, often attributive

thē\ | \krē-ˈā-tiv | \ˈstȯrm\

1. a sudden occurrence of something in large amounts—namely, creativity

2. an alignment of forces that create an event of great intensity

3. a capsule of energy, that is directed and focused

4. a sustained level of committed focus

5. a creative coalescence of art, business and innovation

FOREWORD

THE CREATIVE STORM IS A GAME CHANGER

I have known Nelson Cabral for quite a few years. I first heard him speak at a global conference in Washington, D.C., where to me, he was the star of the show.

As a seasoned executive, managing the technical support arm of Estée Lauder for 17 years, I've been to hundreds of conferences. And truthfully, 99% of the speakers I've heard have failed to leave a lasting impression; whether their content simply wasn't there, they just didn't have anything new to say, or they copied it off Google.

But then you discover a speaker like Nelson, a genuine expert who speaks with authenticity and from a truly different perspective . . . and you realize that he's the real deal. Nelson's presentation stems from genuine innovation, and not only did he show the audience what it is that he does, but how he gets there.

After that presentation I felt truly inspired by Nelson's work, his approach to leadership and his innovation strategies. His presentation got me fired up again, as it wasn't until I heard him speak that I realized that maybe some part of me had lost my way. Nelson helped me become inspired again as a leader. I immediately said to myself "I can't let this guy out of my life"—so I engaged him to work with me. And let me tell you, I'm *so* glad that I did.

What Nelson is doing in *The Creative Storm* is amazing. He is talking about creativity in business, in environments that don't historically value or empower creative leaders.

Nelson explores how leaders can unleash creativity in areas of business where there isn't a lot of investment in people, culture and performance. And what it boils down to is that when you have complex global problems to solve, you need to unleash a *Creative Storm* to solve them.

Once you get past the standard beige and gray way of thinking, pervasive in today's corporate culture, you realize that there's got to be more to people, *more to leaders,* to result in unlocking that human potential. Nelson gets right into that.

In today's business environment, not enough emphasis is placed on how you solve problems. I've witnessed teams struggling with how to improve a product or process, but the answer is so far gone because the culture doesn't allow you to be wrong. So instead of having an innovative culture where you can try new ideas, apply creativity, inspire risk and spark imagination, you have an environment where employees are stifled. We have to, as leaders, do what Nelson says: be the cheerleaders of creativity and innovation. I think that's a game changer.

The turning point and highlight of *The Creative Storm* for me is Nelson's Culture Force 5, "Trigger Collaboration." I think globally, and within companies, people can often end up working in silos. When no one's talking to each other, it's a problem. If you don't have a strong model like the one Nelson teaches, employees and teams will often run off and do their own thing. Operationally, "Trigger Collaboration" is such a great call out—and I think culturally, leaders have to enforce that.

When I unleashed *The Creative Storm* within my teams, I started to get a lot more people feeling empowered.

When you give someone ownership and credit, when you recognize them and spark their imagination, you can just see the light in their eyes. As a leader, we have to remind ourselves that creativity is how great business ideas get started. With *The Creative Storm*, I was truly surprised by how many business-building ideas my team and I came up with to help solve our nagging problems.

The Creative Storm is a game changer. I like that it is a positive disruptive force. Once you start thinking about it, diving in, activating some of his Creative Leadership Forces, you realize how dead your thinking actually is, and how limited your teams and people can become in their silos. *The Creative Storm* really reminds you that at the heart of all great cultures and businesses is creativity.

If you want to accelerate your innovation potential and extract better thinking from yourself and your team, I guarantee you that this book will help you unleash *The Creative Storm* in your business.

Nelson is invigorating, refreshing, inspiring—and simply, a subject matter expert. When you are lucky enough to meet someone who changes your life, and you're smart enough to realize it, you should take advantage of it—and I did.

Thanks to you Nelson. Thanks to *The Creative Storm*.

LAURIE TOSCANO

VICE PRESIDENT, EXECUTIVE DIRECTOR,
GLOBAL END USER SERVICES
THE ESTÉE LAUDER COMPANIES INC.

CREATIVITY REQUIRES STIMULATION AND COLLABORATION, AND YOU, AS THE LEADER, HAVE THE RESPONSIBILITY TO UNLEASH A CREATIVE STORM IN YOUR TEAM.

PREFACE

TO WIN THE FUTURE, BUSINESSES MUST SUMMON THE CREATIVE STORM

Today, many companies are missing that special spark that made them such a phenomenon when they started. That missing spark is creativity.

In fact, many companies are creatively bankrupt. These companies and CEOs face a severe shortage of employees who have the capacity to be creative.

But more importantly, they lack the environment, process and leadership style needed to unearth creativity and innovate.

In today's complex world, innovation is essential in any company that wants to succeed—and the only way to skyrocket innovation is to stimulate it and fuel it with Creative Leadership.

THE ESCALATION OF CREATIVITY

A recent global CEO Study by IBM had CEOs ranking creativity as the most important leadership quality in leaders at all levels. Creativity is now the most critical skill requirement for leaders navigating today's complex business environment. Not just that: 69% of companies report a need for creativity training programs.

BLOW YOUR COMPETITION AWAY

Creativity is what gives your company the business edge it needs. You make this happen by igniting **Creative Leadership**. This is the leadership style of today, right now. The modern leader is embracing it. Future organizational cultures are adopting it. And the Creative Leader is becoming the driver for an organization's talent development.

Once typically found only in creative industry companies, Creative Leadership is now becoming, as a result of the digital transformation, a sought-after management style in *all* industries.

When leaders embrace creativity using **The 9 Forces of Creative Leadership™**, they position their companies for long-term success. Leaders must realize that innovation is the key to an organization's survival, and they have a very important role in building workplaces where people can create and collaborate.

A Creative Leader who instills an inspired creative culture will capture employee performance and engagement and unleash what I call *The Creative Storm*.

If you are looking for a way to get ahead of your competition, the higher-level business creativity of *The Creative Storm* is the way to go. You will blow away the biggest barriers to creativity in your organization, break down walls and bust down any obstacle that's in the way of achieving that next big thing.

In these pages, you will learn how to launch *The Creative Storm* in your organization.

Please do get in touch and let me know how it's going. My email address is *nelson@nelsoncabral.ca* and I would love to hear from you about what you're doing with the ideas in this book.

NELSON CABRAL

MAY 21, 2018
TORONTO, CANADA

NOTE: Throughout the book, you'll find quizzes, checklists and companion tools that can be downloaded, printed and shared with your team by visiting www.nelsoncabral.ca/resources

INTRODUCTION

"When you reach for the stars, you might not quite get one, but you won't come up with a handful of mud either."

— LEO BURNETT

This is a book about a guy who's been driven by a passion for creativity his whole life. As a child growing up in middle-class Toronto, I played soccer, as every young Portuguese boy must (then pitched baseball in my early teens), but sports never interested me. The arts was more my thing—especially in high school. My favorite classes in high school were art and theatre.

While other kids were playing sports, I was in my bedroom singing at the top of my lungs, memorizing lines, rehearsing monologues and painting. It became sort of instinctual. Instead of escaping and rebelling as a kid into booze and girls and drugs, I stayed home and found my escape, finding myself in art and theatre. Staying up all night airbrushing big canvasses was what I loved the most.

And I also discovered a passion for leadership. I found my way to become the Chairperson of the Mayor's Youth Advisory Committee in the City of Mississauga, Ontario, Canada—where I learned public speaking, how to think fast on my feet and how to facilitate meetings. Hanging out with the world's best Mayor, Hazel McCallion, was a thrill and one of the best moments of my life. It was my first experience with leadership, and working within a leadership role.

At the end of high school, I wanted to go to the world-famous Ontario College of Art. I applied, interviewed with my portfolio, and was accepted. But my parents told me I would "never make money in art." So I switched paths and went to the University of Toronto for Political Science and Criminology, hoping to get into Law School because, as my parents told me, "being a doctor or lawyer will make me money."

There was something strange and highly uncomfortable going on during my first year of University. I didn't like it. I was depressed. I realized after a few years that I missed my art and theatre. This feeling continued throughout my university career. I persisted and finished my degree. But at the same time, I needed something to fill that creative gap, so I began performing in community theatre, which to this day will end up being some of the best times of my life.

Well, I didn't get into any law school because my marks were not high enough and I had a panic attack while writing the LSATs (Law School Admission Tests). And I couldn't find a job either, so I went back to school. I got into an "Advertising Copywriting" Program at Humber College in Toronto, which I thought was journalism. I had no idea that I had accidently stumbled upon what would be my career for the next 25 years. "Getting paid to be creative and come up with ideas? I'll take it," I thought.

The ideas and principles in this book first started emerging in 1995, when I got my first job in advertising: winning the prestigious "Leo Burnett Copywriter Internship" at Leo

Burnett in Toronto at Bloor and Church. I didn't realize it at the time, but my experiences there shaped my ideas, beliefs, values and management principles around Creative Leadership, corporate culture and individual creativity.

I began to discover how creative organizations and cultures around them were built. I began to observe techniques and ideas on leading creative organizations, which would continue to be shaped by my experiences later on in my career as a Creative Director, a Commercial Director and Leading Man in musical theatre.

It's here at Leo Burnett Toronto, under the creative direction of cco Martin Shewchuk, that I first discovered (or rediscovered) the power of creativity—the power of Creative Leadership—and the importance of it in my life.

Why a book about Creative Leadership? Because I have noticed from 25 years of working in the creative industries that there are a lot of leaders and organizations able to ignite the highest levels of creativity and innovation—but there are a whole lot more that don't.

In most cases, leaders in creative industries get to the top by starting at the bottom. Many are self-made, meaning that they learned their trade while doing it, not necessarily in a business school. But when someone gets to a point at which they are being considered for a leadership role, are they truly prepared to lead?

In this book, you'll learn how to become a Creative Leader. The first step is to understand the role of *leadership* in sparking and maintaining the highest levels of creativity in your organization. However, leadership skills represent just one set of attributes for the Creative Leader. The Creative Leader also designs and puts in place the right *culture* for creativity. Finally, the Creative Leader fuels high-impact creative *performance* from everyone in the organization.

To master Creative Leadership, you'll learn about the "Creative Leader Superhero Trifecta" of three creative roles—Creative Director, Hollywood Film Director and Leading Man / Woman in a musical—who, respectively, represent the creative attributes of leadership, culture and performance. If you can embody these three roles, if you can ignite Creative Leadership, build a Creative Culture and spark Creative Performance in your organization, you will launch the unstoppable *Creative Storm*.

READY? HOLD ON TIGHT.

LET'S GO TAKE YOUR INDUSTRY BY STORM . . .

PART I

THE ESCALATION OF CREATIVITY & CREATIVE LEADERSHIP

WHAT HAPPENS WHEN YOU ARE CREATIVITY BANKRUPT

WHEN CREATIVITY & COMMERCE COLLIDE

During my two decades as a senior executive and Creative Leader in the industries of marketing, advertising, media, design and entertainment, I have seen agencies, firms, clients, executives and CEOs, in many different industries, frustrated, struggling and stuck in destructive chaos in the hunt for business-building ideas.

I've seen so much wasted time, money and nervous energy coming up with the wrong solutions to brand awareness problems, sales problems, marketing problems, business model problems and innovation problems.

I've seen too many companies hugging the status quo—believing the future would be like the past. And I've been frustrated too many times with the lack of innovative thought in organizations, and thus, the lack of corresponding profits.

WHY YOU NEED METHODICAL INNOVATION IN YOUR ORGANIZATION

WHAT I REALIZED IS THAT LEADERS, MANAGERS AND THEIR TEAMS NEEDED

1. an easier and faster process to solve problems, synthesize solutions and identify business opportunities.

2. a system to produce a bigger catch of valuable business-building ideas—to immediately drive breakthrough innovation and immediately drive high-level employee and operational performance to impact their bottom line.

3. a system that allows them to tap into the creative forces that are stagnant within their employees and organizations. As a business leader, if you can unearth a higher level of creativity, you will drive superior levels of performance and growth and take your company to the next level of success.

As a leader, how can you unearth this higher level of creativity? The answer begins by understanding the secret of *Strategic Creativity*.

THE SECRET OF STRATEGIC CREATIVITY

BUSINESSES—IN THE CREATIVE INDUSTRIES ESPECIALLY— NEED A DISRUPTIVE STYLE OF LEADERSHIP

They are too often driven by art simply for the sake of art. A motive of the highest sort, of course, but not one that generally leads to sustainable growth in business.

Think about all those independent films that usually go absolutely nowhere. The "art for art's sake" fails the business and its public because the motives are fundamentally self-centered and self-interested.

Strategic Creativity is a leadership commitment to enable and select the creativity that produces deliverables.

It requires leaders with the spirit, energy and passion of entrepreneurs.

They master intuition and gut response to make unpopular calls. They will kill ideas that they might like personally because they will not deliver business results. They break the rules and see futures where others do not.

Strategic Creativity succeeds by building tension between creative instinct and operational efficiency.

THE ULTIMATE GUIDE TO INNOVATION VS. STRATEGIC CREATIVITY

Innovation refers to the process of converting an idea into a product or service that builds value customers will buy.

➤ Innovation applies information, imagination and initiative to existing resources.

➤ It delivers something that fills and exceeds customer expectations and business goals.

➤ Innovation is the work of risk-takers and organizations that are in the business of bringing new things to new markets.

➤ Innovation emphasizes process and development, research and technology, competition and methodology.

Strategic Creativity puts the emphasis on creativity, a right brain activity. It puts creativity at the center and describes it as strategic.

> ➤ It effectively places creativity at the service of business thinking and planning.

> ➤ A ruthless commitment to Strategic Creativity ties creativity to achievement, and anchors creativity to insights and research.

> ➤ Creative Leadership frames the projects and paths that deliver a culture of Strategic Creativity.

Strategic Creativity lays the cultural and commercial foundation for innovation and business success. Strategic Creativity also demands a different type of leadership: *Creative Leadership*.

WHY CREATIVE LEADERSHIP NEVER FAILS

Creative Leaders are the *leaders who define and grasp the opportunity to develop a culture of commercial creativity in business.*

Creative Leaders are not the managers who toss ideas around or brainstorm at will and at length, undisciplined, for the art of it. Or develop creative for "creative's sake." Creativity for creativity's sake just can't compete—and doesn't have a place in business.

Creative Leaders methodically drive and disrupt, all based on business strategy. They are leaders and managers who *anchor creativity to business objectives.*

They have developed the skill, ability, confidence and leadership courage to make hardcore business decisions that leverage creativity into commercial success.

2 TIPS FOR HELPING YOU BECOME A CREATIVE LEADER

CREATIVE LEADERS ARE CLIENT-DRIVEN

Creative Leaders are masters in developing Strategic Creativity. They develop trust and loyalty with superiors and clients because they value a forward-thinking, laser-focused creative vision in a business context that is ferociously committed to business-building ideas.

CREATIVE LEADERS ARE CUSTOMER-DRIVEN

The creative entrepreneur will build customer connection with creative business ideas that are anchored to insights and generate profitable growth driven by creativity.

STORM STARTER EXERCISE 1: 41 STUPID REASONS WHY LEADERS REJECT "CREATIVE LEADERSHIP"

Creative Leadership is no longer just assigned to the creative industries. The management approach characteristic of Creative Leaders are now applicable to all industries.

That's because businesses are realizing innovation is the secret to winning the future. No matter what business you are running, you are dependent on ingenuity—and the power of a good idea can transform your future.

Creative Leadership is not new. But it's amazing how many leaders have chosen not to adapt to this style of leadership and management approach.

What's been holding you back from becoming a Creative Leader?

CHECK ALL THAT APPLY:

- ❑ FEAR OF THE UNKNOWN
- ❑ UNCERTAINTY
- ❑ DOUBT
- ❑ INEXPERIENCE
- ❑ LACK OF COMPETENCE
- ❑ KNOW-HOW AND TRAINING
- ❑ MISUNDERSTANDING ABOUT THE NEED FOR CHANGE
- ❑ MISUNDERSTANDING ABOUT THE REWARDS
- ❑ I'M NOT CREATIVE
- ❑ I'M NOT IN THE CREATIVE INDUSTRIES
- ❑ MY PAST
- ❑ THE VOICE OF JUDGMENT [YOU'RE A LOSER!]
- ❑ MY BOSS WON'T LET ME
- ❑ MY HUSBAND WON'T LET ME
- ❑ MY WIFE WON'T LET ME
- ❑ BENEFITS NOT SEEN AS SUFFICIENT FOR THE TROUBLE INVOLVED
- ❑ THAT MEATBALL SANDWICH AT LUNCH
- ❑ A NEGATIVE CIRCLE OF FRIENDS
- ❑ A CYNICAL ATMOSPHERE AT WORK
- ❑ ARCHAIC LEADERSHIP AROUND YOU AND ABOVE YOU
- ❑ CONNECTED TO THE OLD WAY
- ❑ I DON'T NEED TO CHANGE THE WAY I LEAD. I'M ALREADY PRETTY AWESOME WITH MY LEADERSHIP APPROACH AND MANAGEMENT STYLE

- ❏ EXHAUSTION
- ❏ DRUG ADDICTION
- ❏ ALCOHOL ABUSE
- ❏ GREASY FOODS
- ❏ I DON'T WANT TO CHANGE MY ROUTINE. THAT WOULD REQUIRE ME TO DO THINGS DIFFERENTLY
- ❏ PROCRASTINATION
- ❏ NO TIME TO LEARN ANYTHING NEW
- ❏ LACK OF SELF-CONFIDENCE
- ❏ INFLUENTIAL PEOPLE CAN'T SEE HOW GREAT YOU ARE
- ❏ YOUR FAMILY BACKGROUND
- ❏ YOUR ETHNIC BACKGROUND
- ❏ RESISTANCE TO WHAT YOU KNOW YOU NEED TO BE AND DO
- ❏ MOO GOO GAI PAN
- ❏ CHOCOLATE
- ❏ YOUR MOTHER
- ❏ YOUR IN-LAWS
- ❏ YOUR KIDS
- ❏ YOUR SPOUSE
- ❏ YOURSELF

BECOME A CREATIVE LEADER: THE BEGINNER'S GUIDE TO THE CREATIVE LEADER SUPERHERO TRIFECTA

BECOMING A DIFFERENT KIND OF LEADER

"Creative Leadership" is not a passive form of leadership in business, but very much an active process. It's one that inspires employees and colleagues to rise above themselves and achieve greater successes by trying new approaches and taking risks.

CREATIVE LEADERSHIP MADE SIMPLE: THE TRIFECTA

In a nutshell, the three legs of this Trifecta can be likened to the leadership team you would have if you combined the roles of Advertising Agency Creative Director, Hollywood Film Director, and Leading Man / Woman in a first-rate Broadway musical production. That would be quite the awesome dream team.

When all three of these roles come together in one person, and give their best effort, the result can be something truly amazing. But even more importantly, if you want to succeed at igniting Creative Leadership in your organization, you have to have the right mix of Creative Director, Film Director + Musical Theatre Leading Man / Woman entrenched in your managers and leadership.

THE ADVERTISING AGENCY CREATIVE DIRECTOR

The Creative Director in an ad agency is responsible for inspiring the best out of everyone involved, driving the creative strategy and maintaining the agency's standards for creative excellence.

In its best form, this is not simply nagging or browbeating everyone; it should be a process that lights a creative fire within each person and encourages them to achieve something greater than their own individual role.

The Creative Director doesn't push employees—they get employees to take risks and push themselves to loftier heights of creativity and innovation.

Picture the fictitious Creative Director characters Don Draper or Peggy Olson of the television series *Mad Men*— who inspire risk and amplify creativity in everyone around them. What's fascinating is that in 2009, the fictional character Don Draper was named the most influential man in the world—ahead of all real-life figures.

THE FILM DIRECTOR

The Film Director is responsible for creating an atmosphere, climate and culture on a production and set where each participant is inspired to pour everything into making this production the best it can possibly be.

The Director strives to impart his or her vision of the end result, and how that vision can only be achieved when everyone involved rises above the ordinary level of contribution to an inspired level of collaboration.

For this role, think of master film directors and master collaborators Martin Scorsese or Kathryn Bigelow. Scorsese is the great director behind such masterpieces as *Taxi Driver*, *Raging Bull*, *Casino* and *Gangs of New York*, and is universally considered to be one of the most influential directors in Hollywood.

THE MUSICAL THEATRE LEADING MAN / WOMAN

As the most visible person in a top-notch Broadway musical, the Leading Man / Woman must dig deep down within him- or herself and tap into that innermost core of creativity—which in most people, never reaches the surface.

When this person taps into that inner dynamo of creativity, and brings it to the surface in an expression of inspiration that can be seen by all those around them, it can set in motion a wildfire of inspiration and performance.

A great person to visualize in this role is the award-winning and wonderful Nathan Lane or vibrant songstress Idina Menzel—Lane, for his inspired creative work in musicals like *Guys and Dolls*, *The Producers* and *A Funny Thing Happened on the Way to the Forum*, and Menzel for her creative muscle in musicals *Rent*, *Wicked* and *Frozen*.

STORM STARTER EXERCISE 2: THE CREATIVE LEADERSHIP TRIFECTA SELF-ASSESSMENT

As a leader, rate yourself on the following scales, on your ability to be a "Triple Threat Creative Leader":

LEADERSHIP: I inspire risk and amplify creativity like an Advertising Creative Director.

CHECK THE ONE THAT APPLIES TO YOU MOST:

- ❑ NO EXPERIENCE
- ❑ LIMITED EXPERIENCE
- ❑ GOOD EXPERIENCE
- ❑ ADVANCED EXPERIENCE
- ❑ EXPERT

CULTURE: I activate creative cultures and am a master collaborator like a Film Director.

CHECK THE ONE THAT APPLIES TO YOU MOST:

- ❏ NO EXPERIENCE
- ❏ LIMITED EXPERIENCE
- ❏ GOOD EXPERIENCE
- ❏ ADVANCED EXPERIENCE
- ❏ EXPERT

PERFORMANCE: I have the techniques, skills and tools to rediscover and ramp up the unique creative talents in me and my team like a Musical Theatre Leading Man / Woman.

CHECK THE ONE THAT APPLIES TO YOU MOST:

- ❏ NO EXPERIENCE
- ❏ LIMITED EXPERIENCE
- ❏ GOOD EXPERIENCE
- ❏ ADVANCED EXPERIENCE
- ❏ EXPERT

WHAT HAPPENS WHEN YOU TURN ON YOUR TRIFECTA?

The Creative Leadership Trifecta Formula is a catchy little phrase that might sound like some kind of horse-racing scheme to pick winners and make a killing at the track, but it actually refers to real-life business management scenarios.

The "Trifecta" part of the phrase does indeed mean winning in three related leadership categories relative to building, nurturing and managing creativity—and succeeding at igniting Creative and Innovation Leadership, and leading relentlessly creative companies.

By combining these three very different roles into that of a single person, the *Creative Leadership Trifecta Formula* can be achieved by one person and turned loose on the employees of any company.

It's a process that can help you to look at things differently in order to more rapidly find better solutions to the challenges you face.

As a Creative Leader, if you can embody these three roles, you will become a *Creative Leader Superhero* and set the right three conditions to consistently unleash a higher level of creativity. How? By ramping up your Creative Leadership (like a Creative Director), Creative Culture (like a Film Director), and Creative Performance (like a Musical Theatre Leading Man / Woman). That is the key to building and leading a relentlessly creative company.

THE CREATIVE LEADERSHIP TRIFECTA FORMULA:

CREATIVE LEADERSHIP + CREATIVE CULTURE + CREATIVE PERFORMANCE = THE CREATIVE STORM

UNLEASHING THE PERFECT STORM OF PROFITABILITY

When those three weather cells collided in the Atlantic Ocean in 1991 to form "The Perfect Storm," an unstoppable monster of a super-storm was created and unleashed off the eastern shores of the U.S.

If your business leadership can bring the three cells of business innovation together (Creative Leadership + Creative Culture + Creative Performance) using *The Creative Leadership Trifecta Formula*, and generate super-inspiration and collaboration in your employees, you will be unleashing the perfect storm—*The Creative Storm*—within your company, and the resulting culture of creativity and sustained growth will be unstoppable.

The Creative Storm is a proven framework, open system, business process and management approach for inspiring higher-level creativity and innovation in your company.

For a downloadable copy of this framework, tool and exercise, and other companion tools, make sure to visit www.nelsoncabral.ca/resources

CREATIVE LEADERSHIP IS THE BEST WAY FOR ORGANIZATIONS TO NAVIGATE TODAY'S EVER-SHIFTING AND FAST-MOVING BUSINESS UNIVERSE. THE CREATIVE STORM IS HOW TO LEARN IT.

WHAT IS THE CREATIVE STORM?

THE COALESCENCE OF ART, BUSINESS AND INNOVATION

The Creative Storm is a process for those who want to build an unstoppable and engaged creative culture.

By igniting Creative Leadership, building a Creative Culture, and sparking Individual Creativity in your organization, you spur entrepreneurship, increase employee engagement and drive superior levels of productivity and performance.

Only when you introduce the right conditions and climate, and unite the forces, will you unleash *The Creative Storm*—using methodical innovation to manage and kick-start creativity.

WHAT CONDITIONS DO YOU NEED FOR A CREATIVE STORM?

To bring *The Creative Storm* to life in your organization, you need to set the right three conditions for a certain period of time in your organization based on the three "Cells" of Creative Leadership. In short you need:

THE LEADERSHIP CELL

The release of innovation must start at the top.

THE CULTURE CELL

The company culture must embrace, not discourage, creativity and innovation.

THE PERFORMANCE CELL

Each person within the company must have the space and encouragement to release their personal creativity.

When you unleash *The Creative Storm* in your business, your employees will become easy collaborators and fast idea generators. As a skillful group brain, they will collaboratively boost breakout successes.

You will get more groundbreaking work from your teams and organization. And your company will profit from the transformative ideas and landmark innovations those employees produce.

WHAT HAPPENS WHEN YOU BECOME A STORMIN' NORMAN

THE LEADER'S ROLE: IGNITING CREATIVE LEADERSHIP

Creativity at a company starts with leadership—Creative Leadership. You have a responsibility to develop the creativity of your team, push your people to do their best, inspire risk and show their innovative sides.

Creativity also thrives in high energy and positive environments, and it's the role of the creative leader to set the standard and amplify the creativity of everyone around them.

If you stand in front of your team with all the energy and passion of a gentle wind, don't expect a *Creative Storm* to bust out in the lower ranks. You need to exude an infectious spirit, and be uncompromisingly positive and optimistic.

STORM STARTER EXERCISE 3: THE STORMIN' NORMAN SURVEY

How often are you engaged in improving the creativity of your team?

_____

_____

_____

Do you consider yourself a more negative or positive person when it comes to inspiring and developing creativity in your team?

_____

_____

_____

Do you enable the people in your company to communicate with you and each other?

_____

_____

_____

Are you able to trust your gut and follow your own intuition in decision-making? How often do you simply follow logical and expected directions? In what scenarios have you been able to bring together your intuition, logical thinking and opinions of others?

_____

_____

_____

_____

_____

_____

_____

_____

Do you make time for your employees during all phases of the creative process? Do you dedicate time to support them and inspire them? Are you open to discussing ideas with your staff in person? Do you have a process for evaluating and selecting ideas?

_____

_____

_____

_____

_____

_____

_____

_____

_____

_____

WHY YOU MUST BLOW AWAY THE BARRIERS

THE LEADER'S ROLE: BUILDING THE RIGHT CREATIVE CULTURE

It's your duty as a leader to foster a creative culture—but what does that mean?

It means that when your team comes up with interesting ideas, they share those ideas with you and their peers, instead of bottling them up.

It means making sure your team works together and thinks as a team, a collective force, a brilliant group brain—and buys into the idea of a "creative corporate culture."

If a team member knows that their peers will try to steal credit, that their boss won't acknowledge their extra effort, that they'll be ignored from the word "go," you can't expect *Creative Storms* to ignite and turn into innovative content and products that matter to people. Idea improvement must become more important than idea ownership.

STORM STARTER EXERCISE 4: THE CULTURE QUIZ

What do you think about new ideas and innovation in your company? Are new ideas allowed? Is creativity and innovation seen as a bother and not needed or is it seen as a high-level business mandate?

_____

_____

_____

How would you describe your present environment in your place of work, or creative climate? Does your organization have a process for developing new ideas? Who is involved? Is there anyone else who should be engaged?

_____

_____

_____

Do you presently see any barriers in your team or organization that stifle your employees' and team's ability to be creative and innovative?

_____

_____

_____

_____

How often do you lean to that one usual direction and concept right away rather than investing some extra time mining and developing an abundance of ideas? Do you find this automatic knee-jerk response tends to impact your level of success?

How often do you inspire, even urge, your employees to convey new ideas to you? Do they proactively approach you to present new ideas? Are they even allowed? How do you normally respond when staff communicates a new idea to you? What's your typical response?

Are you open to taking some risks using new ideas or new processes? Are you willing to unlearn and proactively forget past success formulas?

UNLEASH STORM TROOPERS LIKE A PRO

THE LEADER'S ROLE: SPARKING PERFORMANCE

Creativity is encouraged and inspired by teams collaborating, and ideas are built upon and added together into coherent goals. However, those initial individual ideas that make up big actionable creative efforts come from individual minds.

You can develop creativity. Like any skill, creativity can be taught.

If your team exercises and your training regimen for new and present staff do not include efforts to bolster individual creativity, you have a problem.

There are techniques, processes and tools that can encourage individual creativity; it's your job as the leader to provide individuals with what they need to achieve superior levels of performance.

STORM STARTER EXERCISE 5: THE PERFORMANCE PROBE

Do you consider yourself a highly creative person? Do you believe you have a high competence in unleashing your own creativity in a business scenario?

_____

_____

_____

_____

What motivates you to get unstuck faster and develop more and better creative breakthroughs? Where and in what state are you most creative? What do you normally do to activate your creativity? Have you taken any proactive steps over the last 6 months to increase your individual creative potential?

_____

_____

_____

_____

_____

_____

Do you use basic creativity tools to produce ideas on your own and with your teams? What creative thinking exercises and techniques do you have in your arsenal? Which ones do you actually apply?

_____

_____

_____

_____

_____

How well do you know your employees? Their traits, strengths, background and passions? Do you know what activates their creativity?

_____

_____

_____

_____

Do you have a group of diverse employees who think differently or do they all think in the same ways?

_____

_____

_____

Do you permit yourself and your team to get out of the office and study your customer—hang out where your customer does?

_____

_____

_____

WHAT IS YOUR CURRENT STORM READING?

SOFT BREEZE OR HURRICANE?

When was the last time you saw a real *Creative Storm* (that unstoppable force of high-level business creativity and innovation) pass through your company's hallways? Do you even know? Do you even remember? Do you even know how to recognize a *Creative Storm* if it smacked you across the face?

If the climate in your organization is tepid and tame, what are you doing right now to make it become something more? Something really big and breakthrough?

The pace of business is too fast for you to just stumble over innovation, or wait for creativity to bubble up naturally.

You need to learn to not just recognize creativity, and not just nurture the creativity you spot, but to inject energy that will ignite and kick-start a *Storm* to put everything your company has ever done before to shame.

STORM STARTER EXERCISE 6: THE CREATIVE STORM RADAR

QUESTION: If we were to track the level of innovation and creativity in your organization, which of the following concepts would describe your current *Storm Reading*:

- ❏ NO WIND
- ❏ COLD FRONT
- ❏ DEEP FREEZE
- ❏ SUNNY
- ❏ CLOUDY
- ❏ THUNDERSTORMS
- ❏ THICK FOG
- ❏ SOFT BREEZE
- ❏ LIGHTING
- ❏ OCCASIONAL HAILSTONE
- ❏ OCCASIONAL DOWNBURSTS
- ❏ HEAT WARNING
- ❏ RAINBOW
- ❏ HIGH WINDS
- ❏ TYPHOON
- ❏ TORNADO / HURRICANE

Why is that?

_____

_____

_____

_____

_____

_____

How could you turn that around?

_____

_____

_____

_____

_____

_____

What's stopping you?

_____

_____

_____

_____

_____

_____

THE CREATIVE STORM IS UNSTOPPABLE.

THE 9 FORCES OF CREATIVE LEADERSHIP

In this book, you will learn how to create the conditions needed for a *Creative Storm* by learning **The 9 Forces of Creative Leadership,** which include three Forces for each of the three *Creative Storm* Cells: Leadership, Culture and Performance.

THE THREE LEADERSHIP FORCES ARE:

- » Champion Communication
- » Release Cheerleader
- » Elevate Strategy

THE THREE CULTURE FORCES ARE:

- » Activate Climates
- » Trigger Collaboration
- » Inspire Risk

THE THREE PERFORMANCE FORCES ARE:

- » Value Empathy
- » Empower Generators
- » Spark Imagination

Pulled together, the first letters of each Force spell the acronym **CREATIVES**.

THE ULTIMATE GOAL AND ROLE OF THE LEADER IS TO:

1. Produce **CREATIVES**: easy collaborators and fast idea generators who are productive as hell and frighteningly efficient, and

2. Unleash a **CREATIVE S(TORM)**

How many forces are you unleashing?

THE NEW ROLE OF THE LEADER:
AWAKEN THE 9 FORCES

F1	**C**HAMPION COMMUNICATION	LEADERSHIP
F2	**R**ELEASE CHEERLEADER	LEADERSHIP
F3	**EL**EVATE STRATEGY	LEADERSHIP
F4	**AC**TIVATE CLIMATES	CULTURE
F5	**T**RIGGER COLLABORATION	CULTURE
F6	**IN**SPIRE RISK	CULTURE
F7	**VA**LUE EMPATHY	PERFORMANCE
F8	**E**MPOWER GENERATORS	PERFORMANCE
F9	**S**PARK IMAGINATION	PERFORMANCE

ARE YOU READY TO FACE A NEW JOURNEY TO FIND YOUR TRUE LEADERSHIP IDENTITY?

UNLEASH LEADERSHIP.

UNLEASH CULTURE.

UNLEASH PERFORMANCE.

PART II

THE STORM WARNINGS: HOW TO IGNITE CREATIVE LEADERSHIP IN YOUR ORGANIZATION

WHEN YOU HAVE THE 9 FORCES FIRING ON ALL CYLINDERS, YOU WILL HAVE SUCCESS

PUSHING THE LIMITS

Isn't it funny how we spend the first couple decades of our lives learning how to follow all the rules without question, only to discover over the next several years that the real key to success usually lies way beyond those borders?

After all, if everyone played it safe all the time, there would be no Leonardo da Vinci, no Marie Curie and no Muhammad Ali. They became great not by coloring inside the lines, but by pushing the limits of what they'd been taught in order to find the pure gold lying just outside that restrictive box.

Whether you're the dynamic CEO of a multi-billion dollar enterprise or a regular Joe Shmoe who crunches numbers all day, there's one secret to maximizing your potential for success: creativity—or more specifically, Business Creativity.

By igniting **The 9 Forces of Creative Leadership** and unleashing ***The Creative Storm*** (that unstoppable force of high-level business creativity and innovation), you can make all the difference for yourself and your organization.

Yet, like any massive burst of dynamic energy, your *Creative Storm* may do more harm than good if it's not released with controlled precision and strategy—and in just the right way.

The key is to cultivate, not decimate, using **The 9 Forces**.

THE ULTIMATE GUIDE TO MODERN LEADERSHIP: HOW THE 9 FORCES OF CREATIVE LEADERSHIP CAN HELP YOU SUCCEED

EMBRACING THE NEW ROLE OF THE LEADER

Growth and innovation in a business is never by mere chance. It is the result of forces working together.

What if you could increase your profitability and productivity by 50% and grow your business by 40% to 100% over the next 12 months?

Leaders who embrace Creative Leadership routinely achieve these kinds of results because they understand high-growth businesses dominate through the constant improvement of The 9 Forces of Creative Leadership.

You need to continually ignite your Creative Leadership by Championing Communication, Releasing Cheerleader and Elevating Strategy.

You need to continually build your Creative Culture by Activating Climates, Triggering Collaboration and Inspiring Risk.

And you need to continually boost individual performance by Valuing Empathy, Empowering Generators and Sparking Imagination.

Leaders and managers need a system that raises employee engagement and taps into their talent's creative potential. Leading from the middle allows workers more freedom and discretion to take the initiative. It encourages more collaboration and communication between employee and manager—and among employees, too.

Such leaders ignite Creative Leadership by integrating and aligning **The 9 Forces of Creative Leadership** in a perfect storm: *The Creative Storm*. And when that strong Creative Leader is present, employees will always know they are in *The Storm Warning*.

Only wise leaders will truly strategically innovate within their businesses using the power of Creative Leadership. It's how you can strengthen your position and take advantage of the changing economy.

The question is: will you be one of them? The Forces at work here are greater than you ever imagined. Get ready to change the way you lead, and amass a fortune—in engagement, performance, innovation and wealth.

THE SECRET OF THE CREATIVE STORM: IT'S ALL ABOUT DELIVERABLES

Although it's impossible to run a business without structured processes, at a certain point you need to cross the gap between business and art.

There's a dynamic tension that exists between creative disruption and operational efficiency, and learning how to navigate that tightrope is essential for boosting your innovation and navigating change.

Unleashing *The Creative Storm* is not about getting all "artsy" and ditching your practical business side. It's about keeping the pressure on and still churning out deliverables—but in more imaginative, original and thoughtful ways. Remember: Business Creativity is not about playing with LEGOs or a room full of Nerf balls, or any of the other off-the-wall exercises you might have run across. **It's about a hardcore business mandate. It's about deliverables, business strategy and pressure.**

CHAMPION COMMUNICATION

STEPPING UP TO THE DANCE OF PERSUASION TO CHAMPION IDEAS

You'd be surprised at how undervalued communication is in the modern business setting.

It's not that communication doesn't take place—far from it! We're communicating on more channels now than ever before: email, texting, instant messaging, social media and video conferencing, to name a few.

The problem is *quality*, not *quantity*. Leaders will spend all day in meetings, or issuing directives to their subordinates through email and text, only to wonder why nothing is done by the end of the day.

But not just any verbal communication will do: nobody appreciates a draconian leader barking orders at everyone in his or her line of sight. Proper communication is a dance of persuasion; the goal is to present your case directly and with confidence, yet avoid imposing your will on your underlings.

Communication has quickly become the new leader's superpower.

IT'S THE DISADVANTAGE OF OUR TECH-ORIENTED WORLD: WE'RE OVER-DEPENDENT ON OUR GADGETS. ACTION—REAL ACTION—HAPPENS THROUGH VERBAL COMMUNICATION.

WHY COMMUNICATION IS THE KEY TO BUSINESS GOAL ALIGNMENT

As the leader of your enterprise, the burden of decision-making is on your shoulders.

This doesn't mean that leaders are stuck doing 100% of the work, but it *does* mean that they're responsible for keeping new ideas and strategies aligned with overarching business goals.

In this way, great Creative Leaders are the champions of communication: their management approaches must both create and direct each new initiative to guarantee that it provides value to the team and organization.

CREATIVE STORM SUCCESS STRATEGY 1: 3 MANAGEMENT HACKS TO BLOW THEM AWAY WITH COMMUNICATION

COMMUNICATION SUCCESS FACTORS

Communication is an art form. It's not always easy, but there are several factors that all great leaders keep in mind as they direct the flow of each interaction:

1. COMMUNICATE YOUR VISION EFFECTIVELY

Communication is critical to the growth of new ideas. However, not just any communication will do the trick. The goal is to present your case directly yet avoid imposing your will on your subordinates.

Great leaders communicate their vision like directors on a film set. Directors have a vision for the endeavor that they relay to their team. Everybody works towards that vision, bringing their own insights to the table, with the directors stepping in when needed to keep the project on course. Creative Leaders understand the goals of their organizations, inform their subordinates about these goals, and make sure that all communications are anchored to business objectives that support the organization as a whole.

2. PROVIDE EFFECTIVE AND PRODUCTIVE FEEDBACK

As a leader, you must be engaged with your team and invested in their success. This means monitoring their progress and providing productive feedback. Giving people regular feedback is key to a Creative Leader's role.

This can be a delicate process, as many workers are sensitive to criticism. Generally, anchoring constructive feedback within supportive comments is a good way around this problem.

Find an effective ratio of praise-to-criticism that simultaneously supports and motivates your team. According to research done by the *Harvard Business Review*, many effective organizations use a ratio of nearly six positive comments for every critical comment.

These numbers will vary based on your individual team, but the bottom line is that leaders must not get so caught up in criticism that they alienate their teams. Be open and respectful with your feedback and be willing to discuss alternatives.

3. ADVOCATE FOR YOUR TEAM

A lesser-known role of leaders is that of diplomat or facilitator. You may find yourself as the liaison between team members or other executives and your shareholders—as the arbiter when disputes arise. As the leader, it's your job to advocate for your team and their ideas. A cornerstone of communication is being able to take your team's ideas and persuade others of their value.

When your team is together and sharing ideas in person, give everyone an equal voice and force people to really listen to each other. Creative Leaders understand that great ideas can come from anywhere—and are willing to champion the ideas of their team when required.

IF YOU WANT TO IGNITE ACTION (AND WIN), COMMUNICATE VERBALLY

As a leader, it's easy to assume that your word is law. Many leaders fall into this trap and fail to provide justifications to those who have to carry out your orders. However, your team won't always see things that way. Great leaders must know how to clearly present their case verbally without steamrolling those who object.

Part of this means staying involved in the day-to-day procedures of your operation. Go to meetings, discuss ideas and concerns with your employees in person, and do what you can do to persuade them verbally instead of overruling them. If you want things to go your way at meetings, go to the meetings.

THE ULTIMATE CREATIVE LEADER MANAGEMENT SECRET: GIVE EVERYONE A VOICE

Golden-ticket ideas can come from any level of your business, and as a leader, it's your duty to make sure these diamonds in the rough make their way to the top and receive the attention they deserve.

If you want to support the growth of new ideas and the highest levels of innovation, you must understand that great ideas can come from anywhere—and you must be willing to champion the ideas and voices of your team when needed and help people communicate.

HOW MANY TIMES HAVE YOU CHAMPIONED AN IDEA YOU DID NOT LIKE?

Your creative team will generate many ideas. As the team leader, you need to champion those ideas. Sometimes you may even have to support ideas that you do not like, but which you realize will ultimately offer value to your organization.

By becoming a Champion of Communication and Ideas, you make it more likely that innovation will be realized.

More importantly, you demonstrate very clearly to your team that not only do you believe in their ideas, but you believe in them, too. And when you choose to advance an idea you're known to dislike, it demonstrates that you're devoted to the team rather than to yourself. This sends a very powerful message to those who work for you.

7 LEADERSHIP TIPS TO HELP YOU SET A NEW "SUPER-PRODUCTIVE TONE" FOR BRAINSTORMING SESSIONS

1. Become a "Guardian of Voices" and protect everyone's unique voice. Specifically go out of your way to coax and get people's opinions, and give them an equal amount of time to be heard.

2. Force people to really listen to each other so they can work together.

3. Encourage yourself and your team to find positive aspects to even the wildest of ideas.

4. Establish a non-defensive setting upfront by reviewing guidelines and ground rules.

5. Accept the fact that it's not your job to tell people "No." But it is your job to make people feel smart and empowered.

6. Enjoy the process and relish in the experience of having vastly different creativity perspectives and styles clashing, interlacing and complementing one another.

7. Help everyone be sensitive enough to make these rough edges mesh together.

STORM STARTER EXERCISE 7: ARE YOU GIVING OTHERS A VOICE— OR JUST LISTENING TO YOUR OWN?

What communication assumptions have been holding you back from this next level of Triple Threat Creative Leadership? Is it time to blow away your beliefs? Here are some clues.

CHECK ALL THAT APPLY:

☐ IT'S NOT ABOUT MY TEAM'S CREATIVITY. IT'S ABOUT MY CREATIVITY.

☐ I WANT TO BE THE ONE TO COME UP WITH THAT NEXT GREAT IDEA.

☐ I DON'T LIKE IT WHEN PEOPLE WANT TO CHANGE MY IDEA.

☐ I DON'T HAVE TIME TO READILY ACCEPT INPUT AND OTHER POINTS OF VIEW.

☐ I DON'T HAVE TIME TO DIRECT, GUIDE, SET UP, CAJOLE AND INSPIRE. IT'S MY TEAM'S JOB TO PRODUCE NEW IDEAS. THAT'S WHAT I PAY THEM FOR.

☐ I FIND IT DIFFICULT TO LOOK FOR THE POSITIVE IN OTHER PEOPLE'S IDEAS.

- ❏ I WILL OFTEN CLING OBSESSIVELY TO ONE SINGLE IDEA—NAMELY, MY OWN.
- ❏ I FIND IT HARD TO REPLACE MY INNER CRITIC WITH AN INNER CREATIVE.
- ❏ MANY TIMES, I WILL THINK OF MY TEAM MEMBERS AS A RIVAL IN A COMPETITION FOR THE BEST IDEA.
- ❏ I OFTEN STRUGGLE TO FOLLOW MY INSTINCTS AND LET MYSELF BE CARRIED ALONG BY SPONTANEITY.

STORM STARTER EXERCISE 8: TAKE THE "GIVE EVERYONE A VOICE" TEST

Write down 3-4 stories where you heard a great idea, but did not take it seriously, or did not consider it.

In each scenario, describe why you did not pick up the idea, develop it further and hand it back—or did not force yourself and other people to really listen.

Share these stories at your next meeting; then ask people to write their own to add to the mix.

_____

_____

_____

_____

_____

_____

_____

_____

_____

_____

_____

GOLDEN-TICKET CONCEPTS CAN SHOW UP AT ANY LEVEL OF YOUR BUSINESS, AND AS A CREATIVE LEADER, IT'S YOUR RESPONSIBILITY TO MAKE CERTAIN THESE DIAMONDS IN THE ROUGH GET DISCOVERED AND PUSHED UPWARD.

CREATIVE STORM SUCCESS STORY: CHAMPIONING COMMUNICATION WITH A LEADING LUXURY CAR BRAND

I had the pleasure of travelling across Canada and helping a leading global premium automaker become more innovative in its best customer experience. The program was designed to help leaders, managers and employees reach and exceed service standards. As an Innovation Catalyst and Executive Facilitator, I delivered a year-long process improvement, leadership development and culture change program that would increase efficiency and accountability, improve services to the public and streamline processes.

Industry surveys had revealed that customers felt the company was not providing the customer experience they expected. Customers had become more demanding and its competitors were driving harder.

To uncover issues around customer service, we engaged with senior executives in executive interviews, staff focus groups, side-by-side process observations and planning sessions. This allowed us to discover root causes around barriers to success. But I didn't just talk to managers and leaders for insights. Here's where the magic happened: I gave everyone a voice and everyone got a chance to talk. I was able to talk to shop mechanics / technicians, back-room parts advisors and floor service personnel. This was the key to our success.

Employees who had never been asked about the company's processes were suddenly part of the conversation. I forced people to really listen to each other. By protecting people's unique voices, we were able to uncover valuable insights and get everyone to work together to come up with collective solutions to achieve higher standards.

Clarity was achieved on what needed work and improvement in the team's day-to-day processes, and there was improved innovation in providing the best customer experience.

STORM STARTER ACTION STEPS: FORCE 1, CHAMPION COMMUNICATION

1. Give everyone an equal voice and require that everyone REALLY listen to each other.

2. Discuss ideas in person with your employees and team.

3. Communicate your direction and vision effectively, and provide helpful guidance and feedback.

4. Know how to advocate for ideas (even those you dislike, but realize they offer value to the organization), persuading others of their value. Present your team's case without steamrolling those who object.

RELEASE CHEERLEADER

EMBRACE YOUR LEADERSHIP RESPONSIBILITY TO INSPIRE RELENTLESSLY

HOW TO CREATE AN ENVIRONMENT THAT MAKES EVERYONE FEEL SPECIAL

English poet John Donne once wrote that "No man is an island." And nearly 400 years later in today's fast-moving business climate, his words still ring true.

One of the lesser-discussed aspects of great leadership involves supporting the team that supports you. You must be their cheerleader. You, as the leader, have the responsibility to keep the passion to create alive in your team.

After all, if anybody needs to be invested in their success, it's you.

Releasing the cheerleader in you is about leaving every team member or employee you interact with feeling better. It's about being a great supporter of people. And it's about keeping people enthusiastic and inspiring them to do even better.

CREATIVE STORM SUCCESS STRATEGY 2: 3 CREATIVE LEADERSHIP LESSONS IN BECOMING AN EFFECTIVE CHEERLEADER

THE THREE KEY CHEERLEADER ATTRIBUTES

1. BUILD ENTHUSIASM

Your primary goal as a cheerleader is to get your workers fired up about their projects.

Those of you who have seen *The Social Network* will remember the scenes when Mark Zuckerberg's crew were still in the early stages of building Facebook. There was a frantic energy to everything they did. Bouts of raucous partying were intercut with periods of being "wired in": a state of total focus and commitment. Zuckerberg knew when to get busy, when to ease up and how to motivate his employees. This type of enthusiasm is what creates dynamic business growth, but it takes a great leader to know when to get busy and when to ease up on the gas.

One way to control what "mode" your company is in is by keeping a clear line of communication. Great leaders keep up with what their teams are doing and show a genuine interest in the latest developments.

Entertain a crazy idea every once in a while. Let your workers get excited. If they view you as a leader willing to listen, they'll be more likely to come to you with their creative (and possibly game-changing) ideas.

2. BE OPTIMISTIC

What's the one thing you never see cheerleaders do?

Sulk.

It's easy to celebrate when things go well. But it's a cheerleader's job to always be positive, even when the other team leads the home team by double its score.

The same is true of your business—when a new marketing initiative fails or you suffer a scathing PR nightmare, it's the leader's job to stay positive and keep morale high.

Challenge yourself to look for the positives when things go wrong and find ways to celebrate both the successes and failures. For as Ellen DeGeneres says, "It's failure that gives you the proper perspective on success."

3. INSPIRE THE TEAM

Through infectious energy and boundless optimism, cheerleaders inspire their teams. And as a great leader, you must do the same.

Sure, this involves staying positive and getting your team invested in their work, but more broadly, it means inspiring them by building their confidence.

➢ Acknowledge credit where credit is due, as this builds trust, respect and honesty

➢ Be honest with your criticism and evaluation

➢ Respect them as members of a team, not cogs in the wheel

➢ Trust them to accomplish their tasks without micromanaging

Support their creativity. Encourage dialogue and free exchange of ideas. Inspiring a team means understanding that each worker has a unique perspective that can add value to your business—and leaders who know how to unlock this potential can help their workers and business achieve great things.

RELEASING THE CHEERLEADER IN YOU IS ABOUT LEAVING EVERY TEAM MEMBER OR EMPLOYEE YOU INTERACT WITH FEELING BETTER.

HERE IS WHAT HAPPENS WHEN YOU CELEBRATE AND PUBLICIZE SUCCESS AND FAILURE

Do you have failure engrained in your corporate culture? Great companies have been built on failure.

Triple Threat Creative Leaders embrace failure because if employees and teams are not allowed to fail now and again, they will never achieve greatness. It's shocking how many leaders still do not stomach, much less encourage, failure.

Triple Threat Creative Leaders know better. They inspire their teams and people to fail sooner, and try again. And they even ensure that failure is celebrated and publicized so that everyone in the organization can learn from the mistakes.

3 TOOLS TRIPLE THREAT CREATIVE LEADERS USE: INTRODUCING "CREATIVE STORM CERTIFICATES OF SUCCESS AND FAILURE"

Have a look at the 3 "*Creative Storm* Certificates of Success and Failure" at *www.nelsoncabral.ca/resources*

They can be used weekly or monthly to give recognition, ownership and credit, and help you achieve higher levels of performance, employee engagement and talent retention:

THE STORMIN' NORMAN AWARD FOR CREATIVE LEADERSHIP

FOR THE CREATIVE LEADER MOST EFFECTIVE AT CONSISTENTLY INSPIRING WINNING TEAMS.

STORM TROOPER OF THE MONTH AWARD

FOR OUTSTANDING INDIVIDUAL CREATIVITY AND UNLEASHING CREATIVE BREAKTHROUGHS.

THE CREATIVE STORM IMPACT AWARD

FOR THE TEAM OR GROUP WHOSE IDEAS
GENERATED CREATIVE DISRUPTION THAT
SPARKED A BUSINESS BREAKTHROUGH.

Use them often!

Simply print them out in your own organization to reward your managers, employees and teams for igniting higher levels of creativity and innovation.

The hidden benefit of awards such as these is as you look at "how" to award them, you're also looking at the factors which measure your *Creative Storms* as a whole.

For a downloadable copy of these "Creative Storm Certificates of Success and Failure," and other companion tools, make sure to visit www.nelsoncabral.ca/resources

Or you can email nelson@nelsoncabral.ca to order your own "Creative Storm Certificates of Success & Failure" and have them mailed to you.

WHY YOU SHOULD CELEBRATE TEAMS AS WELL AS "TROOPERS"

FOCUS MORE ON TEAMS—NOT INDIVIDUALS

When it comes to your "Storm Troopers"—the people actually coming up with these legendary ideas—reward them. BUT, as a leader, you should also be looking at teams rather than individuals. You want to encourage camaraderie and mutual cooperation to maximize the *Creative Storm*'s potential.

Consider setting up an award system, or a number of awards, which reward the objectives you're after. You want your people to be frighteningly efficient and productive as hell, so create awards that measure those things.

CELEBRATE SUCCESS.
BUT ALSO FAILURE.

STORM STARTER EXERCISE 9: MANAGEMENT AS CHEERLEADING CREATIVE LEADERSHIP ASSESSMENT

How often do people from your company share new ideas with you? Do you have time for it? Are you open to it? How do you react?

_____

_____

_____

_____

What do you do when someone from your team is struggling, in a dark phase, or has lost their mojo?

_____

_____

_____

_____

As a leader do you have the traits of enthusiasm and optimism? Do you have a motivational spirit? If so, how you do you unleash them?

_____

_____

_____

_____

_____

Do you make time for "cheerleading" and supporting your people during the stages of the creative process?

_____

_____

_____

How do you presently reward the innovative activities of your employees?

_____

_____

_____

_____

Do you encourage your people to try, fail early and try again? Do you tolerate failure? Even celebrate it?

_____

_____

_____

_____

_____

_____

What are three things you can do starting today to inspire your team more relentlessly?

1. _____
2. _____
3. _____

Write down three stories that represent examples or instances where you were a great cheerleader and supporter of your teams, keeping them enthusiastic and inspiring them to do even better.

1. _____
_____
_____
_____

2. _____
_____
_____
_____

3. _____
_____
_____
_____

CREATIVE STORM CHALLENGE

Over the course of a week you need to "cheerlead" each employee on your team every day. Use an action that is something new, fresh and that brings about an improvement in process, culture or performance.

CREATIVE STORM SUCCESS STORY: RELEASING CHEERLEADER WITH ATLANTIC LOTTERY TV COMMERCIAL SHOOT

I was on set one day for an Atlantic Lottery Corporation TV shoot, where we brought in a director from the u.s. On the day of the shoot, as the crew set up and first scene setup continued, I noticed the Director was barking orders at his crew. His style seemed to be autocratic, top-down leadership. I even noticed a few crew members try and make some suggestions, but he wouldn't listen or take their perspectives into consideration. It seemed to be his way or the highway. He wasn't objectively open to other people's ideas or points of view. His energy seemed to be negative and anxiety filled—no smile, all scowl. From the start, it seemed like the culture on set was an ineffective one.

After he directed a few actors, I noticed we were not getting the performances we wanted. He wasn't a cheerleader or supportive. He wasn't positive, optimistic or exuding infectious energy. We were not able to get usable performances out of our actors. We hit a dead end.

To this day, he is known to me as "The Bad Director."

It was at this moment in my career that I realized I should pursue directing. I realized my passion and expertise in inspiring was exactly what these types of productions needed. One thing I did very well was that I was a great cheerleader and supporter of people. I knew how to keep people enthusiastic and inspire them to do even better.

I ended up co-directing the rest of that shoot and got us back on track.

STORM STARTER ACTION STEPS: FORCE 2, RELEASE CHEERLEADER

1. Establish trust, honesty and belief by giving away credit.

2. Be persistent with your positivity, radiating optimistic, contagious energy, so that you can keep people enthusiastic and inspire them to do even better.

3. Routinely use strategies to keep your team's energy fired up so they never lose their mojo.

4. Give your employees and teams more than five positive comments for every criticism, challenging yourself to identify positive aspects to even the silliest of ideas.

ELEVATE STRATEGY

HOW TO MAKE BUSINESS-DRIVEN STRATEGIC CREATIVITY YOUR GOAL

WHY CREATIVITY SHOULD BE DRIVEN BY BUSINESS GOALS

The creative strategies that Creative Leaders pursue are anchored in concrete business goals. In other words, this is not art or creativity for the sake of creativity. These leaders have a "business reason" for driving creativity and innovation.

Like an improv comedian or an orchestra violinist, Creative Leaders know their art, but are aware that the art is playing a part in something larger at the same time: something strategic, something business-building and something that connects.

MAKING THE RIGHT (AND TOUGH) DECISIONS WHEN THE CREATIVE STORM HITS

One of the key attributes of a Creative Leader is to have the courage to make the tough calls.

They are ruthless with decision-making. They make unpopular decisions for the sake of the work and are always willing to kill ideas they, or their team, love.

IF YOU SUPPORT YOUR DECISIONS WITH DATA, YOU WILL TAKE YOUR INDUSTRY BY STORM

Where would we be without data?

It's funny, but up until the past few decades, the concept of "data" didn't really exist. Now, in the information age, the world is powered by data in all its forms. It truly is the soil where ideas grow.

Data provides context for decision-making. It provides background. And it provides a defensible framework upon which Creative Leaders can explore new ideas.

Naturally, Creative Leaders understand this and use it to great effect.

For example, many bottom-line focused executives may doubt the value of investing in content marketing—it's less direct and less visible than tried-and-true advertisement, after all. However, when you consider the data showing that **80 percent of business-to-business decision makers prefer getting information from reputable articles rather than traditional advertisements**, the value of information becomes clear.

Of course, data comes in many flavors. From business statistics to consumer preferences to audience segmentation guidelines, data cuts through the confusion of decision-making and helps reveal the clearer truth.

Note that it only *helps* reveal the truth. When managed poorly, data can be a double-edged sword, twisted or mis-interpreted in support of the wrong decisions!

THE TRUTH ABOUT DATA, AND HOW TO USE IT WISELY

Be warned, ye who enter here: Big data isn't your magic bullet. Collecting data won't solve all of your problems. Alvin Toffler, noted futurist and author of *Future Shock* may have said it best:

> *"You can use all the quantitative data you can get, but you still have to distrust it and use your own intelligence and judgment."*

Toffler is describing how data alone can be misleading. For all of its benefits, it's a tool, and nothing more. It's up to you, as the Creative Leader, to explore seemingly unrelated data sets and extrapolate insights from them. It can be daunting at first glance, but effective leaders take on the task with gusto and challenge themselves to form connections that others haven't yet seen.

THE CREATIVE STORM SUCCESS STRATEGY 3: 2 GENIUS HACKS EVERY CREATIVE LEADER SHOULD KNOW ABOUT DECISION-MAKING AND DRIVING STRATEGY

1. KEEPING THE SHIP ON COURSE: BE BAMBOO

Great leaders aren't always popular. They aren't best buddies with all their employees. It's not a captain's job to make friends—it's to keep the ship afloat.

In a business setting, this means realizing two things: (1) Brutal honesty and decisiveness are necessary; (2) Neither of these will make you popular. Great leaders are willing to bear the burden of unpopularity for the sake of maintaining a strategy.

That said, there can certainly be too much of a good thing. One of Aesop's Fables tells the story of the oak and the reed: When both are pummeled by a powerful storm, the flexible reed survives while the unyielding oak comes crashing down. So it goes with your business. Strength is a necessary virtue of great leaders, but those who fail to bend with the wind will collapse.

Be like bamboo: strong and firm, but also flexible enough to bend with the winds of change. This is how decision-making skills come into play for Triple Threat Creative Leaders.

As Martin Scorsese once said, *"There is an essence to the creative project you must protect. You cannot make concessions. You've got to lose it, if it doesn't fit character."* So you must be able to make firm decisions and stick to them to ensure the production stays on track.

2. THE BALANCING ACT: INTELLECT, INTUITION & YOUR TEAM

Decision-making is a key feature of every great leader.

Those in power constantly shift between two conflicting ideas: Going with their gut and following the instincts of those around them. This push-pull is present in every business decision, and becomes particularly tricky when working with artists, technicians and specialists who all have their own ideas of how things should be done.

Great Creative Leaders get them working together, and can't afford to neglect the input of the great minds they work with and their own intellect and experience.

THERE'S A FINE
LINE BETWEEN
MICROMANAGING AND
FAILING TO MANAGE,
BUT IT'S A LINE THAT
ALL GREAT CREATIVE
LEADERS LEARN HOW
TO TREAD.

MUST-HAVE CREATIVE LEADERSHIP TIPS TO DRIVE STRATEGY LIKE A PRO

HOW TO BALANCE MICROMANAGING AND MANAGING

Imagine being the priest who stood over Michelangelo's shoulder during the painting of the Sistine Chapel ceiling and said: "*You missed a spot.*" Talk about counter-productive micromanagement!

There's a fine line between micromanaging and failing to manage, but it's a line that all great leaders learn how to tread.

Triple Threat Creative Leaders keep this idea in mind, and accept feedback appropriately while still guiding the wheel of a business's overall strategy:

- ➢ Promote creativity, but reserve the final call.

- ➢ Support independent thought, but don't let the strategy go off course.

- ➢ Encourage risk-taking, but be ready to pull the plug on an idea or direction if the value isn't there.

- ➢ Train and discipline your brain to go from right brain to left brain, so you can make decisions on your team's best ideas "strategically" and put them into action.

STORM STARTER EXERCISE 10: KILLING IDEAS YOU LOVE CREATIVE LEADERSHIP ASSESSMENT

In the space below, do a quick self-assessment on these six characteristics for yourself where you made decisions and unpopular calls for the sake of the work. Jot down 1-2 examples reflecting each quality:

READY:

WILLING:

ABLE:

FAST:

BRAVE:

SMART:

AS MARTIN SCORSESE ONCE SAID, "THERE IS AN ESSENCE TO THE CREATIVE PROJECT YOU MUST PROTECT. YOU CANNOT MAKE CONCESSIONS. YOU'VE GOT TO LOSE IT, IF IT DOESN'T FIT CHARACTER."

THE CREATIVE STORM SUCCESS STORY: ELEVATING STRATEGY WITH NETFLIX TRAILER PARK BOYS CYRUS

I had the pleasure of directing a TV Pilot and mocku-mentary called "Coaching Conversations." The stars were award-winning actors Angela Cullins of *American Sunset* fame and Bernard Robichaud, "Cyrus" from *Trailer Park Boys*. I was very excited to work with such a great crew and a stellar group of actors for a week-long shoot.

As a Director, I try to create an environment where people feel they can flourish and excel. Nobody is oper-ating out of anxiety or fear because I work hard to treat everyone with respect. I'm an easy collaborator and great listener and love to include other people's ideas. I like to know what everybody is thinking and what the challenges and conflicts are.

However, conflict is inherent in a collaborative process. I was having a lot of fun collaborating with Bernie and directing him, as I always want to allow the actor the freedom to create. But he naturally kept falling into his *Trailer Park Boys* "Cyrus" character, who is a bully, rude and unsophisticated. The character he delivered was not in harmony with what I envisioned: a respectful, professional, inspiring President of a company.

Although I loved letting Bernie make choices, and listening to what his thoughts were on story, script and character, at times, I needed to defy him. I needed to make choices that were unpopular, but right for the sake of the work and project. I needed to "be bamboo": flexible enough to bend with the winds of change, but also knowing when it was time to be strong and firm.

STORM STARTER ACTION STEPS: FORCE 3, ELEVATE STRATEGY

1. Be seasoned at candor, brutal honesty and decisiveness, and know when to—and be able to—speak the tough truth.

2. Encourage others to make decisions but defy them when you must, being flexible but defiant, and knowing how and when to rein people in.

3. Be constantly in a balancing act between your intellect (brain and data), intuition (gut) and team—then make your decisions based on this balance.

4. With a strong sense of authority and the courage to make tough decisions, be ready and willing to make unpopular decisions for the sake of the work and business objectives.

ACTIVATE CLIMATES

WHAT EVERYONE SHOULD KNOW ABOUT CREATIVE CLIMATES

WHY THE RIGHT CULTURE SUPPORTS CREATIVITY

What makes a great business? One where employees want to stay? Is it creativity? Innovation? Great marketing? Or is it something more? Is there an "X factor" that ties each together and allows them to build on each other naturally? Enter your corporate climate.

The corporate culture or "climate" of your organization is a function of your company's attitudes, policies and social undercurrents that dictate how ideas grow. This climate can make or break the growth of your business, depending on how it's managed.

Climates dictate whether or not employees come to you with ideas. Climates dictate whether employees feel free to optimize their workflows in new, productive ways. And when taken far enough, climates can even dictate the public's impression of your business.

Just look at tech titans like Google and Apple. These heavy hitters didn't get where they are today from the minds of one or two visionaries (although having a visionary on hand certainly helps). No, their success was created from great leaders who understood the value of corporate climates that encouraged innovation and creativity.

Even from the outside, you can see these climates at work. This constant push has given these tech companies almost cult-like status for their openness and innovative practices.

Clearly, great leaders support cultures of creativity.

As author and noted public speaker Sir Ken Robinson explained:

"The role of a Creative Leader is not to have all the ideas; it's to create a culture where everyone can have ideas and feel that they're valued. So it's much more about creating climates."

YOU HAVE A GOLD MINE IN YOUR ORGANIZATION.

YOU JUST NEED TO LEARN HOW TO MINE.

WHY CULTURE IS MORE IMPORTANT THAN THE LEADER

It's great to have a strong Creative Leader who can whip up a *Creative Storm* and produce some great ideas.

The problem is if that leader goes, the storm dies away.

If your *Creative Storm* revolves too strongly around one person, when they depart, there will be nothing to keep that storm raging. What you really need to do is not just to find an outstanding Creative Leader, but also to build a *Creative Storming* culture.

That's not to say brilliant Creative Leaders aren't valuable, because they really are. If you have someone who's a "Stormin' Norman," you should hang on to him or her for dear life.

The trick is in how you use those Creative Leaders. If they show up and inspire a *Creative Storm*, that's great and you'll benefit, but you'll have no way to fuel it once they're gone.

Instead, you want to use them to amplify everyone else's creativity.

Creative Leaders need to possess surging collaborative and leadership skills, tools and mindset.

They need to inspire a willingness to take risks, to shape a culture of curiosity and inquisitiveness, and to help cultivate collaboration within your company. They should drive your creative strategy rather than being the sole source of creativity themselves.

You need to embrace a creative culture—one that takes action with the results of *Creative Storms*. When you set the conditions for an inspired *Creative Storm* culture, especially with the help of a leader who believes in it and drives it forward, you can have confidence that *Creative Storms* are going to become surging business-building occurrences for a long time to come.

HOW TO BUILD A CLIMATE THAT SUPPORTS INNOVATION

This can be accomplished by allowing ideas to develop past the initial brainstorming. Not all ideas start off ground-breaking, and some require time to mature into their potential. Judging them before they've had a chance to mature can stifle such creativity.

And the only way to do this is to eliminate the creativity killers.

BLOW AWAY THE BIGGEST BARRIERS THAT BLOCK CREATIVITY

Before you can create a culture that unlocks high-level creativity and innovation in your organization, you have to understand the obstacles that hinder or stifle it.

You need to focus in and blow away all the creativity killers in your business.

In a survey by *Fast Company* magazine, one of the world's leading creativity and innovation publications, creative companies and their leaders cited the six big barriers to creativity in business. These are:

1. FEAR OF THE NEW

If you keep slamming the door on every new idea, you'll soon have a company filled with clock punchers who are just there to earn their living. Make sure employees know that even if it's never been done before, your organization is willing to give it a try. One suggestion: start by killing old processes and structures, no matter how effective they may have been in the past.

2. INERTIA

People want to be valued for their work, and giving credit for coming up with a smart business-building idea is a great way to do that. Without a company ethos that focuses on and encourages creativity (recognizing it is vital to growth and profitability), it's going to be an uphill struggle to do away with the barriers blocking creativity—especially since most companies don't measure creativity and innovation on their quarterly reports.

3. BUREAUCRACY

Too many approvals causing delays at every turn? Is top management isolated? Are you and your management team standing in your own way and don't even know it—stifling creativity instead of encouraging it? When ideas appear, think about how you and others treat them. What you're looking for is enthusiastic treatment that applauds the originator of the idea, but works collectively to build on and improve it. A *Creative Storm* won't ignite or sustain itself in a rigid system, or with rigid leaders that stifle ideas. The best indicator of an ideal environment for a "creative culture" is evidence of collaboration, a free flow of information and leaders and employees who are eager to improve on others' concepts for breakthrough content and products.

4. QUARTERLY PROFIT DEMANDS

There is often a perceived corporate need to report a continuous stream of quarterly profits. When managers are
too hyper-focused and obsessed with short-term thinking,
then can undermine long-term thinking that big innovation normally needs. This challenge means leaders will
favor quick marketing fixes and cost cutting over quality
innovation and process.

5. CONFLICTS WITH OTHERS

It's natural that leadership and conflict go together. If you
can't address conflict in a healthy way, get out. The key is
to embrace it and not fear it. Developing effective conflict
resolution skill sets is key. Understanding communication
and emotions, and being able to pick your battles, avoid
conflict and define behavior standards is crucial.

6. OFFICE POLITICS

According to some sources, 47% of workers feel office
politics take away from their productivity. Be prepared to
stick to your principles, but also accept that you won't win
every battle. Focus your persuasion on the gatekeepers, and
build your case to accommodate political realities. Identify
the "tough" players and learn how to be politically sensitive.

These barriers are formidable, but finding ways to break them down and to ensure they don't reassert themselves is critical.

Work hard enough, for long enough, with enough enthusiasm, and your efforts will yield results and crash through these barriers to creativity and innovation.

THESE BARRIERS ARE FORMIDABLE, BUT FINDING WAYS TO BREAK THEM DOWN AND TO ENSURE THEY DON'T REASSERT THEMSELVES IS CRITICAL. BE A BARRIER BREAKER.

BANISH BUREAUCRACY, OR ELSE

IF YOU HAVE A RIGID HIERARCHY, YOU HINDER PROGRESS AND INNOVATION DIES

One of the most common storm barriers is the presence of a rigid hierarchy, bureaucracy and command structure in an organization.

The bosses seem to stay up out of the fray—and the more power they have over the organization, the less they seem to engage.

Whatever new ideas do appear are handed down from on high, without rationale or sharing between regular employees—or even a willingness to look at ideas from outside the company (co-creating content and products with customers).

Even worse, employees don't have any process, flexibility, permission or encouragement to challenge or question bosses' decisions and wants.

This type of behavior has a lot of negative outcomes that go beyond creativity (including employee morale, engagement, happiness, productivity, faith and trust in management, etc.), but it is creativity—which is so import-ant to your business—that is most seriously damaged by this sort of hierarchy.

If lower-ranking employees don't have the ability to put forward their own ideas, not only could you be missing out on all kinds of insightful possibilities, but they'll be unenthusiastic about implementing any ideas.

After all, creativity and that next big landmark innovation can come from anywhere, and anyone, at any time.

WHY CULTURE ACTIVATION DEMANDS CREATIVE STORM BUY-IN

Free exchange of ideas is vital, but it won't mean much if it's not partnered with a company ethos that does something with those ideas.

An organization that runs on inertia or is comfortable with hugging the status quo could get a dozen industry and market-changing ideas a day, and still be left behind.

Even if there's no institutional bias against new ideas, if nothing is ever done with them, what incentive does anyone have to come up with them?

To get the buy-in from all levels of your company, make creativity everyone's responsibility. Show them that creativity is a core business mandate and that it goes hand in hand with gaining an advantage and ensuring success.

Ensure that they understand why you are implementing *The Creative Storm* and how it benefits them, their teams and their future. Tell them that thinking outside of the box generates passion and excitement. Remind them that when team members have a say and are involved in the creative process, there is not just massive engagement, but "connection"—the number one human need that activates the heart.

Philippe Starck said, "We are responsible for our creativity. It's a duty." And ideally your employees will feel the same way.

STORM STARTER EXERCISE 11: YOUR CREATIVITY BENEFITS WISH LIST

Question: Which of the following benefits and amazing results of a creative climate are most important to your organization?

- ❑ INCREASED ENGAGEMENT

- ❑ INCREASED STAFF MORALE

- ❑ INCREASED PASSION

- ❑ INCREASED PROBLEM SOLVING

- ❑ INCREASED PERFORMANCE AND PRODUCTIVITY

- ❑ INCREASED INTERACTION

- ❑ INCREASED MOTIVATION

- ❑ INCREASED TEAM BONDING AND COLLABORATION

WHY YOU MUST CHECK YOUR EGO AT THE DOOR

As we know, the best ideas rarely come from the highest levels of an enterprise. These days, innovation occurs at every level, from C-Suite executives to interns to customers. And as our once-linear corporate strata continues to evolve, leaders must be prepared to accept ideas from any place they might arise, and not assume that only top managers have the answers or ideas.

The key to innovation is to be open to new ideas no matter where they come from.

This is the secret to building an innovative corporate climate: Always be listening, always be open to new ideas, be willing to engage over ideas, and always be pushing your team to ask questions.

As a Creative Leader, it's not your job to come up with the ideas, but provide just the right setting for teamwork, risk taking and collective creativity—as well as personal growth and fulfillment.

CREATIVE STORM SUCCESS STRATEGY 4: ALLOCATE BUDGET AND TIME TO CREATIVITY

Even when you've changed your performance review schemes to account for *Creative Storms*, employees might find it hard to really get into coming up with new and original ideas.

They still have deadlines to meet and plenty of other responsibilities. Even if one employee can make the time to storm up some new ideas, the key ingredient of collaboration would be nearly impossible as their colleagues are still busy.

This can be resolved by allocating budget and time to creativity and innovation—allocate time and resources to "storming"—so you build an inspired creative culture with a Creative Leader that believes in it and drives it.

You must deliberately allocate time and budget to thinking about new ways to be more efficient, new ways to connect with and attract customers and be more loved by clients and stakeholders. You need to create a system where time is explicitly set aside for every employee to work on creativity and innovation.

With this time allocated to storming, employees will not feel pressed by their ordinary obligations and will instead be free to concentrate on kick-starting a *Creative Storm*.

If you've implemented the right organizational changes and conditions, and provided the right Creative Leadership, you should be able to see a great storm in the making from far away—and be ready to capitalize on the surge of creativity and innovation.

In addition, when you issue that *Storm Warning*, the whole organization will be fired up for something special—and want to help ignite and spur on the idea to perfection.

STORM STARTER EXERCISE 12: YOUR CREATIVE LEADERSHIP STORM BARRIER ASSESSMENT

Question: Which creativity killers presently exist in your business? Select your biggest barriers to creativity and innovation:

- ❑ FEAR OF THE NEW

- ❑ INERTIA

- ❑ BUREAUCRACY

- ❑ QUARTERLY PROFIT DEMANDS

- ❑ CONFLICTS WITH OTHERS

- ❑ OFFICE POLITICS

What are you presently doing to be a barrier breaker and blow them away? Be as specific as you can:

_____

_____

_____

_____

What's stopping you?

_____

_____

_____

_____

_____

_____

TITANS LIKE GOOGLE AND APPLE DIDN'T GET WHERE THEY ARE TODAY FROM THE MINDS OF ONE OR TWO VISIONARIES. THEIR SUCCESS WAS CREATED BY GREAT LEADERS WHO UNDERSTOOD THE VALUE OF CORPORATE CLIMATES THAT ENCOURAGE INNOVATION AND CREATIVITY.

CREATIVE STORM SUCCESS STORY: ACTIVATING CLIMATES IN A "CREATIVELY BANKRUPT" ADVERTISING AGENCY

I was once hired to be Executive Creative Director of an advertising agency to get them to the next level creatively. The first thing I needed to do was take an audit of the organization's leadership, culture and performance.

What I found were multiple "barriers" in the company that stifled and grounded *Creative Storms*, including over-managing, micromanaging, extreme bureaucracy, inertia, fear of the new and more. In short, this agency had no creative soul.

There was no sense of "creativity" as it wasn't in the fabric of the agency. Creativity wasn't celebrated. And worst of all, there wasn't any Creative Leadership. That concept had never been part of the company's mandate.

The solution was to reframe creativity in order to produce a better pathway. I began to raise expectations, standards and the quality of the work. The only way to meet these standards was to encourage collaboration and embrace creativity rather than throw up barriers to it.

I also introduced new creative techniques and processes that helped demotivated, underperforming superstars. For example, I launched a monthly creative awards show at this company called "The Nellys."

Eventually my efforts yielded results: more collaboration, more innovation and new ideas, stronger culture and engagement—and most importantly, bigger profits.

STORM STARTER ACTION STEPS: FORCE 4, ACTIVATE CLIMATES

1. Create a culture where everyone can have ideas and feel that they're valued, celebrating both success and failure.

2. Know how to recognize and blow away the "TOP 6" biggest barriers to creativity in business—and ensure they don't reassert themselves. Protect your teams from hostile environments and clear the obstacles from their paths.

3. Don't hover, judge or criticize while your teams are working, because that leads to underperformance and underthinking. Recognize when you, or other managers and leaders, are creativity killers.

4. Volunteer the best questions and ignite a culture of curiosity—keep on inquiring, keep on probing, keep on learning.

TRIGGER COLLABORATION

IF YOU THINK LIKE A CLOCK TOWER, YOUR BUSINESS STRIKES IT RICH

When it comes to your business, every piece is essential.

It's kind of like a clock tower, when you think about it. You have a service or a product (the clock face) that provides value to your market, with a thousand cogs and springs and screws working behind the scenes to keep it running.

Business owners get so caught up in perfecting their "clock face" that they neglect the care of the delicate mechanisms that allow it to function: employees. At times, leaders don't see them, but without the value they offer, your business can't function.

When employees come together as a team, there's no limit to what they can build.

CREATIVE LEADERS REALIZE GOOD IDEAS AREN'T RELEGATED TO JUST LONE SUPERSTARS, BUT RATHER COME OUT OF COLLABORATIVE EFFORTS.

THE TRUTH ABOUT TEAM DYNAMICS

WHY TWO HEADS ARE BETTER THAN ONE

Like a clock tower, collaboration between each part of your business is essential to the success of the enterprise. But unlike a clock tower, businesses are far more dynamic: the cogs of your system can, and should, think independently.

Collaboration between employees is essential to success. And while there's value in them thinking independently, collaboration is a cornerstone of steady growth. Two heads are better than one, as the saying goes, and the same goes for creating better products. Multiple minds, when working together in functional and coordinated ways, almost *always* create a better product than a single mind working alone.

Creative Leaders realize good ideas aren't relegated to just lone superstars, but rather come out of collaborative efforts.

HOW TO USE THE THREE C'S TO ACCELERATE COLLABORATION

How can we start to co-create effectively? How can we enlist the people we work with and those we're trying to reach out to? How can we pull them all into the creative process?

To achieve this type of value-driving collaboration, Creative Leaders utilize the three C's of effective team dynamics: Communication, Coordination and Cooperation.

➤ Communication involves sharing messages and information among the group.

➤ Coordination is about organizing activities to help team members work efficiently.

➤ Cooperation is powered by group members working together towards a common goal.

With these three concepts acting as collaboration benchmarks, great Creative Leaders should strive to support these initiatives any way they can.

THE SECRET TO BUILDING THE STRUCTURE FOR STRATEGIC CREATIVITY

HOW THE HORIZONTAL STRUCTURE IS MAGIC

People once worked where their fathers worked. They saw themselves on a lifetime path. They kept their noses to the grindstone or worked at climbing ladders to significant management positions. Some made the climb and some did not.

Your business, like many other operations, is dealing with that legacy. You see it in large complex organizations that are locked into a vertical structure. The structure itself creates inertia as the layers of bureaucracy slow decision-making.

A horizontal structure is more inviting for creative professionals and the businesses they support. They think less of ladders and more of space at different levels where they can collaborate. And, it is your job, as Creative Leader, to create that collaboration-inducing environment, space and climate.

WHY COLLABORATION REQUIRES FREEDOM

In school, *collaboration* meant chipping in, sharing information and exchanging assignments.

In the creative business, *collaboration* refers to an openness of space and mind.

As a Creative Leader, you can build that nurturing environment by exploiting space.

Creatives share a passion for working on the floor, over pizza or around the coffee machine. They prefer lounge chairs to office chairs and might even pick the beanbag chair in the corner.

4 MANAGEMENT HACKS THAT WILL HELP YOU IGNITE COLLABORATION

How can you, as a Creative Leader, add to the physical environment? Here are 4 management approaches you MUST utilize to spur on collaboration.

1. You develop a climate of collaboration when you let team members offer ideas in a no-fear climate and coach them to accept criticism, revision and refusal.

2. You mentor staff so they stay self-confident but learn to self-assess.

3. You help employees realize their ideas are not the best simply because they created them.

4. You let team members take ownership only after their contribution has been vetted by the group.

2 COLLABORATIVE CULTURE STRATEGIES THE BEST CREATIVE LEADERS USE

As the captain of the ship, it's the leader's duty to create organizational strategies that support collaboration. With the 3 principles of team dynamics (communication, coordination, cooperation) in mind, leaders have plenty of opportunities to build this collaborative culture:

1. Propose regular "town hall" meetings where all team members can freely contribute ideas. It doesn't matter if they're the receptionist or the CFO: Great ideas can come from anywhere, and lower-level employees will need to be given opportunities to share their thoughts.

2. Encourage debate and critique of each proposed idea. No idea should be accepted into the corporate playbook without scrutiny. Push the members of your team to voice their concerns and opinions in safe environments.

Innovation can come from anywhere, but it's up to the Creative Leader to enable his or her team to collaborate and bring this innovation to life. But collaboration can also bring challenges—namely, establishing ownership over shared ideas. This notion of "taking credit" for ideas is toxic to a collaborative business environment.

IMAGINE INSTEAD A WORKPLACE WHERE NO EMPLOYEES CARED ABOUT HAVING OWNERSHIP OVER AN IDEA. EACH WORKER COULD TAKE AN IDEA, SHAPE IT, EXPERIMENT WITH IT AND SEND IT BACK FOR GROUP REVIEW WITHOUT WORRYING ABOUT WHO CONTRIBUTED WHAT.

THINGS I WISH I HAD KNOWN ABOUT IDEA OWNERSHIP

THE POWER OF RELINQUISHING OWNERSHIP

Some people take it personally when their ideas are criticized, so they hold back proposing them. Creative Leaders know this is a poison to the creative environment.

Imagine instead a workplace where no employees cared about having ownership over an idea. Each worker could take an idea, shape it, experiment with it and send it back for group review without worrying about who contributed what.

Doesn't that sound like a workplace where more creativity will occur versus one where people fiercely defend their ideas from external influence? Instead of sticking to the outmoded concepts of idea ownership, leaders should replace them with something more conducive to cooperation.

HERE'S WHAT HAPPENS WHEN YOU RELINQUISH IDEA OWNERSHIP TO THE GROUP

By placing the creative responsibility on the group rather than the individual, it creates an atmosphere where group members don't worry about who contributed what and don't feel defensive about criticism of particular ideas.

Think of this as *idea improvement*. Any suggestion becomes the immediate property of the group, and is the launching point for team-oriented problem solving that takes everybody's perspectives into account.

Each proposal is separate from the individual, so people aren't held captive by clinging to ownership of ideas. Ideas can be reviewed, challenged and scrapped, without worrying about offending the person who proposed it. Responsibility of ideation transfers from an individual to the group, creating an open environment.

It's this separation of the individual from the idea that allows your workers to discard their inhibitions and let their creativity flow. When workers are encouraged to share and contribute without fear of retribution, you'll find that the diversity of viewpoints and ideas will go into overdrive.

Idea Improvement versus idea ownership must be engrained in your culture.

CREATIVE STORM SUCCESS STRATEGY 5: AMPLIFYING CREATIVITY IN EVERYONE YOU WORK WITH USING PHRASES THAT IGNITE, NOT STIFLE

How can you become a **Storm Trooper** that inspires collaboration and ignites action?

Use these storm-summoning empowering phrases to bring on like-minded Troopers to kick-start your next *Creative Storm*:

CREATIVITY INSPIRING PHRASES: 10 WAYS TO BECOME AN EASY COLLABORATOR

"There's something there."

"I like that."

"We could also . . ."

"That's interesting."

"Yes, and . . ."

"What if . . . "

"Keep talking. Tell me more."

"Why not?"

"That's a neat idea."

"How could we . . . "

If you want to lead your employees to new heights, as the new **Stormin' Norman,** you need to cultivate collaboration and keep the storm raging.

....

These storm-preventing killer phrases will downgrade your next *Creative Storm* and make your organization creatively bankrupt.

Avoid these creativity-crushing phrases at all costs:

CREATIVITY CRUSHING PHRASES: 10 WAYS TO STIFLE CREATIVITY AND INNOVATION

"We can't do that."

"We don't have the budget."

"Client will never go for it." / "Leadership will never buy into it."

"That's a good idea, but . . . "

"That won't work."

"That's crazy."

"We already tried that."

"We don't do it that way here."

"Yes, but . . . "

"I don't like that idea."

For downloadable Posters of these "Creativity Inspiring" and "Creativity Crushing" Phrases and Cheat Sheets, and other companion tools, make sure to visit www.nelsoncabral.ca/ resources

STORM STARTER EXERCISE 13: LEADER AS COLLABORATION (AND CREATIVITY) KILLER

Write down three scenarios / projects in recent memory where you used **Creativity Crushing Phrases** prematurely to kill an idea or stifle creativity and innovation in a person or team:

_____

_____

_____

_____

_____

Write down some **Creativity Inspiring Phrases** you could have used to approach the scenario / person / team differently to ignite a _Creative Storm_:

_____

_____

_____

_____

_____

CREATIVE STORM SUCCESS STORY: TRIGGERING COLLABORATION WITH PRO•LINE SPORTS LOTTERY

The concept of collaboration as opposed to selfishly hanging on to idea ownership brings me back to an earlier point in my career when I was the Advertising Copywriter for Pro•Line Sports Lottery in Toronto. I was tasked to put together a new brand and marketing campaign.

The client wanted to try and veer away from the expected and conventional "sports enthusiast" brand concept. My Art Director partner and I developed a TV spot concept where two aliens walk into a bar, walk up to the counter, and ask the bartender to switch the TV to their favorite sporting event. They travelled across the galaxy to catch the game.

When I presented this idea to our Account Director, he laughed and said, "Love it! Their cable's out!" Now at this stage in my career, I had an ego, so I didn't really think about his idea of aliens with no cable or working TV. I always wanted to be the one to come up with the idea. For me, in those early days, it was all about idea ownership and "getting credit."

I went to bed that night, and continued to incubate on the creative. When I woke up in the morning, I realized how brilliant that line was. That was a turning point in my career: I left my ego at the door and replaced "idea ownership" with "idea improvement." I realized by having that line at the end of the commercial, as a subtitle on the screen, "OUR CABLE'S OUT", as the alien speaks "alien," made the TV spot more unexpected and memorable, and thus, more effective.

The Pro•Line *"Bar Hopping Aliens"* TV spot won first place, "Best TV Spot in Canada", in Playback Magazine's TOP SPOT AWARDS. Plus, Sport Select sales exceeded the original plan of $200MM fueled by a +7% growth of the Pro•Line business.

STORM STARTER ACTION STEPS: FORCE 5, TRIGGER COLLABORATION

1. Commit to replacing "idea ownership" with "idea improvement"—grabbing ideas, developing them further, then handing them back.

2. Accept that you don't have to be the one to come up with all the ideas; know how and when to stop clinging obsessively to one idea—namely, your own.

3. Foster an environment where innovation and new ideas are not only safe, but encouraged and expected—creating structures, time and spaces where ideas can be discussed and collaboration can flow. Give everyone, regardless of his or her position, the opportunity to be heard.

4. Co-create future products, services and processes with employees, customers and external partners, staying open to engaging those willing to play in a "test lab" environment.

INSPIRE
RISK

IF YOU FEAR THE NEW, YOU'RE DEAD IN THE WATER

WHY RISKING FEARLESSLY AND RATTLING CAGES LEADS TO SUCCESS

"A person who never made a mistake never tried anything new."
— **ALBERT EINSTEIN**

You tell 'em, Einstein.

Aside from the obvious "get to work" interpretation, the Father of Relativity was giving us a warning: we can't let our fear of failure stifle our creativity.

To make an impact in today's business world, creativity is essential. In fact, whether in business or not, creativity is one of the most powerful forces in the world. There are few limits to the human imagination, and when our boundless brilliance is combined with enough blood, sweat and tears, great things can happen.

Unfortunately, most of us never achieve these lofty dreams.

Why?

Fear. **Fear stifles creativity.** We're a species that thrives on comfort and familiarity. We don't like risk.

WHY BUILDING CREATIVE COURAGE IGNITES INNOVATION

WHY WE ARE TAUGHT TO AVOID RISK

As a society, we're pushed to avoid risk at all costs. You can see this trend in every industry out there—risk management consultants, threat analyses, damage control plans; these all speak to a fundamental fear of making a mistake. What if our risk doesn't pay off? What if we lose money? Or worse yet, look dumb in front of our associates?

Creative Leaders need to take charge of their teams and flip the script on what it means to be a "risk-taker." If Gates and Jobs had both played it safe and stuck it out through college, the technological landscape as we know it today would probably be unrecognizable.

Great risks can yield great rewards. And you, as a Creative Leader, must instill the confidence in your workers that enables them to take risks with their projects.

It might sound scary, even counterproductive to your time-tested business model, but this is where we have to challenge the traditional paradigm of risk as something to hide from. Instead, think of risk as a journey of exploration. Everything in the corporate strategy guide, all of the best practices, basically everything on the map that's already filled in, that's old territory. Working within known territory frees you from the burden of risk, but also prevents you from exploring what benefits are hidden in those uncharted corners of the map.

It's in these uncharted corners that Einstein, Gates and Jobs found their success.

Is your business next?

CREATIVE LEADERS NEED TO TAKE CHARGE OF THEIR TEAMS AND FLIP THE SCRIPT ON WHAT IT MEANS TO BE A "RISK-TAKER."

CREATIVE LEADERSHIP MADE SIMPLE: CREATE THE FIRST DISRUPTION

HOW SMALL RISKS-BIG TARGETS IS THE ANSWER

The very definition of creativity is veering away from the norm—bypassing the dull, expected targets and going after the unexpected instead.

Using the same dependable methods you have always used will keep on delivering the exact same boring results.

While reliable is nice and all, predictability is not what inspires either your employees or your clients. Hugging the status quo won't get you to the future first.

Go after the big targets instead: invest in low-risk ideas to start if you have to, but get out there and just start doing.

CREATIVE STORM SUCCESS STRATEGY 6: INTRODUCING "THE NELSON TOUCH" CREATIVITY FRAMEWORK

THE ULTIMATE GUIDE TO INSPIRING RISK

My understanding of Creative Leadership, innovation and risk-taking was originally born in the school of disappointment.

After working with status quo-hugging creative companies, corporate brands and Fortune 500 organizations around the world, I became frustrated with the lack of innovative thinking and corresponding profits I saw in their businesses. I became inspired by the energy and desire to innovate, and frustrated by the inability to turn that motivation into concrete action-plans.

So I set out to challenge leaders, teams and organizations to question the status quo and consider disruptive strategies of innovation. I invented a "creativity framework" and process that allows individuals and teams to generate and evaluate ideas along a spectrum of creativity and spectrum of risk.

Clients began embracing my new risk-taking creativity framework. Since my inspiration, Creative Leadership and involvement on business projects yielded breakthrough innovation and superior levels of creativity and team performance, they called this process "The Nelson Touch."

QUANTITY OVER QUALITY: WHY "MORE PLEASE!" NEVER FAILS

Studies have found that when a team is engaged and working on creative projects, it's more advantageous to focus on getting an abundance of ideas rather than focusing on finding the one "winning" idea—at least at first. Landmark innovation and breakthrough creativity demands lots of exploration, a wealth of ideas, which is why your goal should be to increase your potential choices.

Therefore, these are my expectations as a Creative Leader leading a team towards innovation:

I inspire and expect my innovation and creative teams to develop 30 solutions to every challenge, conceptualizing 10 ideas for each "Nelson Touch" category.

THE 3 NELSON TOUCH CATEGORIES ARE:

➤ **HALF NELSON:** This is what I call 50% level creativity, where ideas are literal, expected, passive, safe and status quo or conventional.

➤ **FULL NELSON:** At this creativity level, you are being 100% creative with your ideas, and concepts are lateral, unexpected, assertive, smart and unconventional.

➤ **LORD NELSON:** This is where you start to rattle some cages. Here, you are reaching a 200% creativity level, and ideas are Lazarus (come alive, thought lost but resurrected, raised from the dead), very unexpected, perhaps aggressive, risky and far-out.

This 3rd category, "Lord Nelson," is where the magic happens. It is based on Lord Admiral Horatio Nelson, a famous British officer in the Royal Navy, known for his leadership style and innovative ideas for winning sea battles. This is where the most disruptive, inspired and unexpected ideas live.

"The Nelson Touch" Process forces you to break through conventional wisdom, to go far beyond small, incremental changes by connecting with exaggerated thoughts and "stretch goals." By pushing yourself to the edges, you'll consider ideas you would not have previously considered and uncover fresh, new ideas.

Once you acknowledge and audit the status quo, you can then ignite a steady stream of disruptive strategies and unexpected solutions to stay ahead of the game—and discover your "Lord Nelson" ideas.

STORM STARTER EXERCISE 14: DISCOVERING YOUR "LORD NELSON" BUSINESS-BUILDING IDEA

When it comes to generating solutions to a problem you are facing, you should always think about quantity over quality—at least at first.

Name a project, issue or business problem you are attempting to find a better solution for today.

_____

_____

Use the worksheets on the following pages to assemble enough raw ideas for each of the three "Nelson Touch" categories that could solve your challenge.

Make sure you find 10 ideas for each level of creativity, as that is the only way you will dig down deep to where the newest, most unexpected ideas can be found. And avoid evaluating your ideas too early.

For a downloadable copy of "The Nelson Touch" Creativity Framework and Idea Generator Worksheet, and other companion tools, make sure to visit www.nelsoncabral.ca/resources

HALF NELSON

50% CREATIVITY

CREATIVITY THAT IS:

- ➤ Literal
- ➤ Expected
- ➤ Passive
- ➤ Safe
- ➤ Status quo / Conventional

1. _____

2. _____

3. _____

4. _____

5. _____

6. _____

7. _____

8. _____

9. _____

10. _____

FULL NELSON

100% CREATIVITY

CREATIVITY THAT IS:

- ➤ Lateral
- ➤ Unexpected
- ➤ Assertive
- ➤ Smart
- ➤ Unconventional

1. _____

2. _____

3. _____

4. _____

5. _____

6. _____

7. _____

8. _____

9. _____

10. _____

LORD NELSON

200% CREATIVITY

CREATIVITY THAT IS:

- ➤ Lazarus
- ➤ Very Unexpected
- ➤ Aggressive
- ➤ Risky
- ➤ Far-out

1. _____

2. _____

3. _____

4. _____

5. _____

6. _____

7. _____

8. _____

9. _____

10. _____

ONCE YOU ACKNOWLEDGE AND AUDIT THE STATUS QUO, YOU CAN THEN IGNITE A STEADY STREAM OF DISRUPTIVE STRATEGIES AND UNEXPECTED SOLUTIONS TO STAY AHEAD OF THE GAME—AND DISCOVER YOUR "LORD NELSON" IDEAS.

CREATIVE STORM SUCCESS STORY: INSPIRING RISK WITH INVEST NEW BRUNSWICK

One day, there was a project that came across my desk for Invest New Brunswick, a government Crown Corporation responsible for attracting investors and business. My assignment was to develop a new marketing and brand concept to persuade corporations to relocate and expand their businesses in New Brunswick, Canada.

I decided to try something new with my team and client: I introduced them to "The Nelson Touch," my idea generating framework and innovation methodology. We focused on quantity over quality and getting more ideas rather than getting better ideas, at least at first. My team and I generated 30 concepts along my spectrum of creativity: 10 "Half Nelson" ideas, 10 "Full Nelson" ideas, and 10 "Lord Nelson" ideas.

When we presented our ideas to the senior account team, they began to kill any ideas that were risky or unconventional—or beyond the norm of "government." I insisted we consider all ideas. "But the government would never approve that! It's too risky," they said. I encouraged them not to reject ideas simply because the client had never produced something like that before. "Why not blaze new trails, challenge norms and stay open to new ideas?" I asked.

We presented ideas to our client and the client bought into a "Lord Nelson" idea, which we called "Where Business Comes, Naturally." Using nature and New Brunswick wildlife as a canvas, unique "spokespeople" were developed to represent the province's workforce. Business professionals with animal heads allowed us to communicate the strong characteristics of New Brunswick's workers—including mailing bobble head figurines to decision-makers. This highly unexpected and innovative idea resulted in more awareness, more conversations with prospects and more businesses relocating to and expanding in New Brunswick.

STORM STARTER ACTION STEPS: FORCE 6, INSPIRE RISK

1. Push yourself, your team and your clients out of your / their comfort zones to challenge assumptions and disrupt the status quo, forcing yourselves to look at ideas you wouldn't have previously considered.

2. Encourage your team to use established conventions as the starting point to drive innovation and change—using "The Nelson Touch."

3. Employ "creative destruction" to achieve new success, kill old processes and unlearn and selectively forget past success formulas, no matter how effective they had been in the past.

4. Know how to experiment and test ideas in a safe way, without damaging your brand. Start with small projects and small budgets, then test, learn and prove.

VALUE
EMPATHY

WHY FALLING IN LOVE WITH THE PEOPLE YOU'RE CREATING FOR NEVER FAILS

As a Creative Leader, you and your team must be encouraged to gain a much deeper understanding of your customers and how you can connect to their lives using your content, product or services. In doing so you will identify new areas of opportunity.

Many times, Creative Leaders must encourage their teams to put aside their egos, roles and expertise and simply listen, be humble, and as one of my favorite bands, Depeche Mode, sings:

> *"Keep the same appointments I kept.*
> *Try walking in my shoes."*

Be curious about what it's like in their shoes.

Simply, have empathy.

This is the only way a team and business can unearth the right problems to solve, and then identify and create super innovative offerings that present the right solutions.

Empathy helps boost customer satisfaction, increase customer loyalty and ultimately drive new revenue. Empathy leads to the insights you need to grow your business.

THE ART OF INSIGHT MINING & NEED FINDING

Creative Leaders must be very creative, and able to generate ideas for stories, backgrounds, music and other elements involved in creative industry productions. One of the ways to do that is, through empathy, to immerse yourself in your target audience.

This is usually the first stage in the larger art of creating products that customers love and that satisfy brilliantly.

Highly successful and effective innovation often builds on consumer analysis and insights and then shapes them into breakthrough products and services. In the process, they also differentiate the companies that produce them, for these companies are able to inspire, provoke, validate and entertain.

WHY YOU NEED TO UNCOVER UNARTICULATED NEEDS THROUGH EMPATHY

By carefully researching end users *before* they start developing design concepts, creative professionals can uncover customer needs and wants, including the needs that the customers may not even realize they had. (No traveler in the 19th century ever said they needed automotive transportation. Yet the automobile was an innovation that obviously responded to customers' needs.)

If you want your organization to become the next Google, Apple, Tesla, Alibaba, WhatsApp, Facebook or any other company that you greatly admire (and who wouldn't?), then you'll definitely want to implement this principle: Customer insight must be expanded to discover *unarticulated* customer needs.

STORM STARTER EXERCISE 15: "I DON'T THINK I KNOW MY CUSTOMER WELL ENOUGH" CHECKLIST

Question: Have you and your team asked yourselves these questions lately?

- ❏ WHERE ARE MY BLIND SPOTS WHEN IT COMES TO MY CUSTOMER?

- ❏ HOW DO I KNOW IF MY IDEA IS GOOD?

- ❏ WHAT WOULD MY DREAM CUSTOMER TESTIMONIAL SAY?

If not, then why not?

_____

_____

_____

_____

YOUR HIGHEST PRIORITY IS TO SATISFY THE CUSTOMER THROUGH EARLY AND CONTINUOUS DELIVERY OF VALUABLE PRODUCTS AND SERVICES.

UNLEASHING YOUR COMMUNITY IN CONVERSATION: 4 QUESTIONS

BE OPEN ENOUGH TO HAVING CONVERSATIONS IN THE MARKETPLACE

When customers and stakeholders can see your product or service (or a prototype) with their own eyes, touch it with their own hands, and experience it with all of their senses, then they can give you the meaningful feedback you need, enabling you to learn the most about what's ultimately going to work and what won't.

1. Does it work the way you intended?

2. Will it change the customer's life?

3. What is appealing and what's not appealing?

4. What needs to be improved?

CREATIVE STORM SUCCESS STRATEGY 7: 6 WAYS TO HELP YOU UNDERSTAND YOUR TRUE VALUE TO YOUR CUSTOMER OR CLIENT

1. Identify internal stakeholders and external clients who are willing to play within a 'test lab' environment.

2. Stay informed about new markets and emerging technologies.

3. Follow blogs, trendspotters and websites reporting on your product or industry.

4. Sift through publications in your product or content's ecosystem.

5. Explore market research and data.

6. Be curious. Get out of your office. Go hang out where your customer does.

9 QUESTIONS THAT WILL HELP YOU MINE FOR INSIGHTS

1. What is right with your product?

2. What is wrong with your product?

3. Who is your target audience?

4. Should you target somebody else?

5. Who is NOT supposed to use your product or like your content?

7. What business are you in?

8. Should you be in another business?

9. What is the turning point and moment of truth for your customer?

Used properly, these questions can trigger you to uncover great insights that will lead to effective innovation.

3 GENIUS LEADERSHIP HACKS TO FIND MASSIVE VALUE FROM EMPATHY

HOW TO INTEGRATE EMPATHY INTO YOUR STRATEGY, PROCESSES AND DATA COLLECTION

Leaders can use empathy in numerous ways to derive these valuable insights:

1. **Enhance Decision-making / Defend The Big Idea:** One of the most common uses for empathy and insight mining is to enhance strategic decision-making. When reviewing a new idea, initiative or strategy, be sure to also review the relevant insights you have at your disposal. Each decision should be backed by consumer insights that can provide a framework for how the strategy will produce benefits for you and your team.

2. **Support and Fuel Creativity:** Use empathy to accelerate your creative process. Review trends and consumer habits that have been effective in the past, and then brainstorm how you can bring them into your organization's structure. Can you integrate old marketing strategies with social media? Are there new software systems that let you analyze consumer preferences in

greater detail? Can your story and characters be strengthened by some new cultural or lifestyle trends? Let the unearthed insights guide your creative processes.

3. **Optimize in Real Time:** Data flows are never ending and provide a constant stream of information that leaders can use to optimize their projects. Rather than waiting on reports each week, month or quarter, big data gives you a real time assessment of your industry and lets you customize strategies on the fly. Optimization means efficiency. Data can help you get the most out of your project and produce a stronger ROI.

The insights gained from these types of empathetic, customer-centric applications allow leaders to push their businesses beyond their competitors. Follow the trends in your industry by tracking forward-thinking sites and blogs. Get a team together and sift through as much market research data as possible to identify trends, priorities and emerging concepts that you can put to work.

There's a term used for leaders who succeed with these kinds of analyses: *Visionaries.*

STORM STARTER EXERCISE 16: THE STORM STARTER EMPATHY CHECKLIST

HOW TO TRANSLATE UNSEEN NEEDS INTO INNOVATIONS

❑ UNCOVER YOUR TOP 3 INSIGHTS.

❑ IDENTIFY THE TOP 3 TRENDS.

❑ UNEARTH THE TOP 3 PRIORITIES FOR YOUR CUSTOMER, IN CONTEXT OF YOUR INNOVATIVE IDEA OR PRODUCT.

❑ MAKE 3 REALISTIC PREDICTIONS FOR YOUR CUSTOMER'S FUTURE NEEDS.

❑ PREDICT 3 UNREALISTIC, BUT DESIRED, IMPLICATIONS FOR YOUR CURRENT CUSTOMER.

❑ PREDICT 3 IMPLICATIONS FOR YOUR CURRENT BUSINESS / INDUSTRY.

CREATIVE STORM SUCCESS STORY: VALUING EMPATHY WITH GE

When I was lead copywriter for our client, GE, there was an exciting project where an endless search for consumer needs resulted not only in an effective breakthrough campaign, but a Cannes award-winning TV commercial.

My Art Director and I were tasked with coming up with a brand campaign concept for the launch of the new GE Handi•Hite Fridge in North America. This is a fridge that has the fresh food section on the top and the freezer on the bottom—unlike traditional fridges.

After getting briefed on the project, we went away and started developing ideas. My starting point for every brand challenge was to get as much information about the product as possible—digesting lots of info. This allowed me to more freely get ideas flowing.

But even more successful for me was immersing myself in the target audience—which I always found was what ignited my best ideas. An insight stood out for me: women, the key decision-makers in appliance purchasing, were frustrated that the section they use most, the fresh food section, was not at the perfect height. So in a perfect world, if women could turn the fridge upside down, there would be less bending.

Thus, the idea was born: in all advertising, Mrs. Jones would be seen lifting a fridge single-handedly and turning it upside down. This North American-wide campaign turned sales upside down and put the GE Handi•Hite on back order for two years.

CREATIVE LEADERS
MUST ENCOURAGE THEIR
TEAMS TO PUT ASIDE
THEIR EGOS, ROLES AND
EXPERTISE AND SIMPLY
LISTEN, BE HUMBLE, AND
AS DEPECHE MODE SINGS:
"BEFORE YOU COME TO
ANY CONCLUSIONS, TRY
WALKING IN MY SHOES."

STORM STARTER ACTION STEPS: FORCE 7, VALUE EMPATHY

1. Encourage yourself and your team to use market research, staying informed about new markets and emerging technologies, and follow blogs, trendspotters and websites reporting on your product or content's industry—because that's the soil where ideas grow.

2. Proactively put yourself and your team(s) in your customer's shoes, staying open to and encouraging you and your team to getting out of the office and hanging out where your customer does.

3. Know how to leverage empathy to enhance decision-making, defend The Big Idea and support and fuel creativity.

4. Be open to dialogue and discussion in the marketplace, fostering open innovation and allowing you to listen to the wisdom of your customers.

EMPOWER GENERATORS

THE TRUTH ABOUT DEVELOPING & NURTURING TALENT: CREATIVITY CAN BE TAUGHT

Don't operate under the principle that there are a chosen few out there who are unusually brave, exceptionally creative or are otherwise special snowflakes who are capable of more—more fearlessness, more innovation, more creativity—than others.

That assumption simply isn't true.

The idea that you can't train creativity or develop your creatives does not hold up to the evidence. Whether you ask the top Creative Leaders in the field or researchers at the universities, they'll tell you the same thing: creativity is a skill, one we can nurture.

Creativity isn't "you've got it or you don't." Every single individual possesses creativity that can be leveraged into something truly exceptional.

WHY CREATIVE LEADERS ARE GREAT COACHES

Leadership positions in creative enterprises are too often filled by people who have not been trained for the position or in the required leadership skills, tools and mindset.

In most cases, leaders in creative industries get to the top by starting at the bottom. They are often selected and promoted because they are a top creative *performer*, but not necessarily a top "Creative Leader."

Many are self-made, meaning that they learned their trade while doing it on the job, not training for it in business school.

But when someone gets to a point in which they are being considered to lead in a creative company, are they truly prepared to lead? If Creative Leaders want to more effectively manage creativity and creatives at a higher level, they must learn how to empower people to become outstanding idea generators.

In other words, you might have gotten promoted to leadership by showing you can score lots of goals. But once you become a leader, you have to let go of being "the player" and remind yourself that you are now the leader, the "coach."

It's your job to direct, guide, set up, cajole and inspire— to give your team all the information and clues they need to solve the problem at hand.

Your #1 job is to help others score goals and make them stars.

WHAT HAPPENS WHEN YOU REMOVE THE BARRIERS OF FEAR

Everyone's terrified of what they don't know and the status quo seems nice and safe when compared to the risk of putting yourself, or your business, out there—only to fail.

As a Creative Leader, and business leader, you need to blow away the barriers of fear and inertia so these employees can unleash their creative potential.

You need to focus on enabling a creative culture where your team feels supported and engaged, allowing them to more fearlessly tap into those creative resources.

One way to free the wealth of creative ingenuity from its suffocating trap of fear and doubt is to let your team know that failure will not be punished. That doesn't mean that failure should be encouraged. Although failure is the foundation upon which many successful companies are built, sometimes encouraging people to fail does not deliver success.

Yes, cushion the fall when failure happens, but what should be specifically encouraged is *trying*. Encourage the process rather than focusing only on the outcome.

Play around with small pilot programs to promote gravitational interest and exploration without fear of risk or expectation of reward.

Not trying is always a larger risk than failure could ever be.

WHY YOU SHOULD ALWAYS START WITH QUANTITY

As a Creative Leader, you need to expect quantity over quality—at least at first.

Research shows that when a team is engaged in creative work, it's actually better to focus on getting more ideas than getting better ideas, at least at first.

Why is quantity better than quality? Because a focus on quality can shut the team down. The higher the expectations for a high-quality product, the more closed the group becomes. They self-censor more. They worry that their ideas aren't good enough and so they don't bring them up. As a result, there is less of an abundance of ideas to choose from.

To shake up your own team, challenge them to produce more.

HOW MANY TIMES HAVE YOU VOLUNTEERED TECHNIQUES AND ASKED GREAT QUESTIONS?

Your value as a Creative Leader shouldn't be limited to only spotting inefficiencies and blocks; you need to help your team build creative embers to a roaring blaze.

You need to cultivate your own extensive inventory or library of creative techniques and exercises. Learn the myriad tactics others use, then suggest the ones that fit the task or specific employee at hand. And learn to ask the best questions.

After you have provided that spark, move on and light more storms.

CREATIVITY ISN'T "YOU'VE GOT IT OR YOU DON'T." EVERY SINGLE INDIVIDUAL POSSESSES CREATIVITY THAT CAN BE LEVERAGED INTO SOMETHING TRULY EXCEPTIONAL.

HOW DIVERSITY IN ALL ITS SHAPES, COLORS AND FLAVORS HELPS BUILD CREATIVE CULTURES

It's been said that creative geniuses aren't people who think of wholly original ideas, but rather those who combine previously unrelated concepts in unbelievable ways.

As a Creative Leader, you must recognize each member of your team as a unique combination of traits, a unique piece to be used to drive innovation. Only when you understand what each piece offers can you leverage them to their maximum potential.

In many ways, your ability to observe talent means more for your ability to drive innovation than your personal creativity. If you can identify and leverage the strengths already present in your team in a new way, innovation will arise as a natural consequence.

CREATIVE STORM SUCCESS STRATEGY 8: 3 WAYS LEADERS CAN USE DIVERSITY TO BREED CREATIVITY

1. LEVERAGING UNIQUE INDIVIDUALS

When asked, skillful leaders consistently report one secret to effective leadership: leveraging the strengths of team members. In any field where creativity plays a critical role, it behooves leadership to identify the strengths and individual driving forces of each member of the team.

THE CHESS BOARD: SKILLFUL MANAGERS AS CHESS PLAYERS

Leadership in innovation must be more akin to grandmasters playing chess than children playing checkers—the pieces all move differently in chess, but this allows for a richer end result, with exponentially greater depth and potential.

Then to master leadership, like in chess, you must master the pieces. As an exercise, ask yourself what you really know about each individual team member—what tasks they excel at, what they struggle with, alongside whom they work best.

2. SKILL INVENTORIES

The sort of understanding that begets true innovation and exceptional team management requires effort to develop. That means maintaining an inventory of your team members' unique skills, traits and motivators.

The more granular you can make your inventory the better: if you have a team member who excels on a short leash but underperforms on a long one, that's a critical detail that can mean the difference between a successful team and a failure. The key is to build on people's strengths and provide support for manageable weaknesses.

3. DIVERSITY AND THE MELTING POT

Remember the checkers versus chess comparison earlier. This becomes all the more relevant when you consider, beyond the strengths we considered earlier, the type of pieces you're playing with, or rather, the backgrounds— cultural, professional and personal—of your employees.

Creative innovators consistently see improved results from diversity, as a team full of competent individuals with unique perspectives will find more effective and efficient paths to success.

Start paying more attention to background diversity. Paying attention to cultural, professional, economic, ethnic or academic differences can help you in building strong, diverse and high-performing teams.

3 MANAGEMENT HACKS TO UNLEASH SUPERIOR LEVELS OF PERFORMANCE & PRODUCTIVITY

Do you want to ramp up your own individual creativity and that of your team members? If you or someone on your team needs a jolt of creativity, these tips will fire up your energy and creative problem-solving skills.

1. ME-TIME AND WE-TIME

A good Creative Leader needs to encourage team members to use time wisely. That means accepting the value and necessity of "Me-time" and "We-time." Most studies show the best creative environments arise when individuals generate alone and nurture together—in other words, me-time first, we-time second.

Always allow for "me-time" to generate and storm ideas (immersion, incubation, illumination) before meeting with your team to share ideas, for "we-time."

2. TIME MANAGEMENT AND BUILDING A PROCESS

Of course, effective generation of ideas needs to happen on a schedule if you want to drive innovation. If your creative minds frequently run head-first into roadblocks due to flawed processes, you'll lose the momentum you need to drive ahead of the pack.

That said, you truly can't rush genius. What you should do instead, as a Creative Leader, is to suggest improvements. Don't impose, as the creative process must be personal to be worthwhile. But if you spot inefficiencies and blocks from your vantage point as an outsider, you can nudge your team members in the right direction and help them clean up the way they navigate creativity.

Don't focus on what works for you, or works for a particular approach to creating; as a Creative Leader, you want to understand the full breadth of possibilities.

One basic and dependable creative thinking process that can be suggested is one created as long ago as 1962 by Graham Wallas in *The Art of Thought*. Based on his study of renowned creators, he suggested a 4 stage model for creativity, also known as "The 3 I's":

I. **Immersion**: Collection of information. Read, research and immerse yourself in the challenge.

II. **Incubation**: Turn your mind off, stop thinking about it, transfer the problem to unconscious and let it do the work for you.

III. **Illumination**: Return to the challenge with a fresh perspective, and ignite a sudden inspiration or intuitive revelation, that 'eureka' moment.

IV. **Verification**: Use a rational process to
evaluate.

You can recommend a more organized process, a focused
approach, or a messier, more spontaneous one. But always
remember to encourage your team to turn off creativity, so
they can turn on creativity. Getting away from a project
and experiencing something new and different can inspire
new thinking.

3. PHYSICAL ENVIRONMENTS

It's important to understand the non-cerebral aspects
of creativity as well, if you want to generate generators
that can get the job done. Consider the old standby, the
lightning bolt of insight that comes not hunched over a
desk, not in the wakeless hours of the night, but in the
shower the next morning. A change of space can have an
immense impact on the way your team functions.

This leads some teams to open work environments.
Many companies will like a tight team, everybody in one
room, so ideas feed off of each other.

But remember, alone time is also crucial to the process. Instead, it's best to allow your team to find its own
equilibrium, to take input from your creative minds and
apply your own understanding of team members to set
the ideal stage for creation. And from time to time, shake
things up—just to see what it knocks loose.

THE TOP 5 BEHAVIOR CHARACTERISTICS CREATIVE LEADERS MUST MANAGE

A common misconception sees creative people sitting in circles and tossing nerf balls until something sticks. In fact, creative people are very driven in ways that are not easily managed.

The renowned developer of positive psychology, Mihaly Csikszentmihalyi, identifies some key behavior characteristics Creative Leaders must manage:

1. Creatives have a biorhythm that alternates between intense work and periods of idleness. They enjoy the flow of their work but do not like schedules.

2. Creatives are at once smart and naive. There is no evidence that creatives have high IQs, but they demonstrate what analysts consider a certain emotional and mental immaturity. They can move from one angle to another, generate a lot of ideas and make original associations and connections between ideas and perspectives.

3. Creatives try to balance responsibility and irresponsibility. They like play, but playfulness does not go far in a business—so creatives also demonstrate endurance and perseverance, and thrive under pressure to produce deliverables.

4. Creatives tend to be imaginative and struggle with relevance to their current reality. Their job explores the fantastic, but work happens in the real world.

5. Creatives seem extroverted and introverted but generally prefer one or the other. They may move from one modality to the other with or without awareness.

These characteristics present both a challenge and opportunity for Creative Leaders who want to unlock the floodgates and unleash the productive, commercial and business-building innovation and energy of *The Creative Storm*.

STORM STARTER EXERCISE 17: UNCOVERING BEHAVIOR CHARACTERISTICS IN YOUR TEAM

Write down 3-4 stories or examples where one or more of your employees have shown these top 5 Behavior Characteristics:

_____

_____

_____

_____

_____

_____

_____

_____

_____

_____

_____

_____

_____

_____

_____

_____

_____

_____

AS A CREATIVE LEADER,
CONSIDER YOURSELF
THE "EYE OF THE STORM."
THIS IS THE REGION OF
CALM WEATHER AT THE
CENTER OF STRONG
CYCLONES—BUT IT'S
ALSO WHERE THE STORM
GETS ITS ENERGY.

HERE IS WHAT HAPPENS WHEN YOU BECOME "THE EYE OF THE STORM"

TURNING CREATIVES INTO CREATIVE LEADERS

As a Creative Leader, consider yourself the "Eye of the Storm." This is the region of calm weather at the center of strong cyclones—but it's also where the storm gets its energy.

That's you! The force that ignites *Creative Storms*, launching your employees not only to heights of creativity, but also to heights of Creative Leaders themselves, inspiring and guiding others.

After you have ignited one *Creative Storm*, move on and unleash more storms. The magic here lies in employees who embrace your inspiration, and spur on even stronger *Creative Storms*. That is, they become Creative Leaders in their own right.

In the *Harvard Business Review*, there was an article I read called "How to Ignite Creative Leadership in Your Organization." It discussed how Creative Leaders excel at creating Creative Leaders. Creative organizations don't just have one Creative Leader running the show; instead, they have "Stormin' Normans" directing their energy towards igniting Creative Leaders, or "innovation ambassadors" throughout their organization.

Creative Leadership is all about "Proactive Leadership," and inspiring the next generation of leaders in your organization.

STORM STARTER EXERCISE 18: YOUR EYE OF THE STORM AUDIT

As a Creative Leader, the "Eye of the Storm," you need to ignite *Creative Storms* in your people by encouraging risk and embracing failure. You need to be the protector and champion of new ideas. You need to lead the charge in pushing the envelope in your people and pursue even higher highs. That means after you've provided that spark in someone, you move on and light more storms.

Name 3 people in your organization, or on your team, whom you recently empowered or in whom you unleashed a *Creative Storm:*

1._____
2._____
3._____

Name 3 people in your organization, or on your team, whom you could work harder to nurture and spur on to achieve higher levels of performance:

1._____
2._____
3._____

CREATIVE STORM SUCCESS STORY: SPARKING GENERATORS WITH SABIAN CYMBALS & GRAMMY AWARD-WINNING MUSIC ICONS

Not only was I Creative Director for SABIAN, the world's #1 cymbal company, I also had the opportunity to travel the world and direct the world's best drummers and percussionists in DVDs, documentaries, TV Commercials, Films and Videos. We'd bring together the world's best drummers and percussionists, in world-renowned music cities, and let them unite and rave about the best cymbals in the world.

But I knew this would not be easy. Nurturing trusting and respectful relationships is never easy—especially with very different artists, together in one place.

I needed to give up on the concept that treating everyone the same will work in motivating and inspiring creativity. I found that if I could recognize their differences and unique qualities, I would be able to better orchestrate their talent.

My goal was to understand and discover the unique strengths of each talent, like in a chess game. I took a creative inventory of each person's skills, talents and communication styles, to make sure I understood where they were coming from. I got really clear about it. Then I would assemble the right skills and talents for each scene. Plus, I catered to strengths. Certain people responded well to having a long leash, some wanted healthy competition, some wanted trial by fire.

One musician would get angry whenever I started to give him instructions. He did much better when given a long leash. Other musicians didn't mind direction, but needed competition to bring out their best. For example, at times I would give two drummers the chance to be the lead for one of the videos. Not only did this bring out great brotherhood and camaraderie, but also better performances.

STORM STARTER ACTION STEPS: FORCE 8, EMPOWER GENERATORS

1. Volunteer and inject your unlimited arsenal of creative techniques into your employees and teams regularly, suggesting—but not necessarily forcing—a process.

2. Urge your employees to turn their minds off so they can turn creativity on.

3. Embrace a melting pot attitude: recognize and capitalize on skills and traits of employees and accommodate to strengths, believing that diversity in all its shapes, colors and flavors helps build creative cultures.

4. Magnify the creativity in everyone you come into contact with, making retention and talent development a conscious choice.

SPARK
IMAGINATION

THE INTERNAL STORM: IT STARTS WITH YOU AND IS IN YOU

WHY YOU NEED TO TAKE CARE OF YOUR OWN CREATIVITY FIRST

Creativity is a vast source of energy that flows within all of us. Every individual has the power to tap into it and use it to enhance their own lives and inspire others.

Whether you want to use creative energy to tell stories, write music, produce films, invent technology, design fashion, create future-forward buildings or develop hundreds of other imaginative projects, all you need to do is free your mind and develop skills that can be refined over time.

Everyone has incredible creative potential. If you think you're too inflexible or Type A to be creative, well, stop waiting for some other guy or gal to come along and be creative for you.

Business creativity and innovative cultures starts with *you*. And every Creative Leader not only needs to facilitate creativity in others, but also needs to learn to unleash the creative potential in themselves.

EACH OF US HOLDS AN INCREDIBLE CREATIVE FORCE INSIDE—ONE SO POWERFUL, THAT ONCE RELEASED, A WORLD OF THOUGHT AND WONDER NEVER BEFORE IMAGINED IS REALIZED. I AM HERE TO TEACH YOU HOW TO UNLEASH THAT CREATIVE FURY IN ORDER TO SHAPE THE FUTURE YOU WANT.

CREATIVE STORM SUCCESS STRATEGY 9: WHY IT'S NOT JUST ABOUT YOUR TEAM'S CREATIVITY, IT'S ALSO ABOUT YOUR CREATIVITY

SET STANDARDS BY MODELING CREATIVITY

Some scholars and business experts have suggested that Creative Leadership has nothing to do with your creativity and everything to do with your team's creativity. I completely disagree.

While most Creative Leaders are responsible for mentoring and managing the talent, the best Creative Leaders also get involved in the work. It's all about leading by example.

When your teams see you getting your hands dirty and developing ideas as well, they learn to respect your leadership and what you do. When you make a decision or offer feedback, your team will be more likely to follow and champion your leadership because they see you experiencing the process every day.

Train yourself to be exceptionally creative: it will set a good example for your teams' members. By setting high standard ideas alongside your team, you will ignite your teams to reach for the stars as well.

Your effectiveness as a Creative Leader will ramp up significantly if you learn to be a creative genius and ignite your own internal *Creative Storm.*

THE SECRET TO UNLEASHING YOUR CREATIVE STORM: DON'T GROW UP!

Ask a room of kindergarteners what they want to be when they grow up, and you'll get a long list of outrageous, fantastic, thoroughly impractical answers.

A Ballerina, Inventor, Astronaut, Comedian, Spy or NHL All-Star.

Not one kid in the room will say he wants to be an accountant, or she wants to be a business executive. This is because kids have one thing that most grown-ups lost somewhere along the way: imagination.

When you were a kid yourself, every game you played was fueled by this wonderful, powerful stuff. Children use imagination to make up stories, to surprise, to delight, to progress—but most importantly, to create.

When's the last time you felt a sense of wonder?

When's the last time you imagined yourself doing something that made you purely happy without stupid practicality coming in like a big wet blanket to quench the flames of your dreams?

If you can't answer either of those questions, you shouldn't be surprised that your creativity has gone into deep hibernation out of sheer necessity.

You're starving your creative spirit to death. You're creatively bankrupt.

THERE ARE TWO MAIN REASONS THAT MOST KIDS DON'T GROW UP TO BE BALLERINAS, INVENTORS, ASTRONAUTS, COMEDIANS, SPIES OR NHL ALL-STARS, AND THEY'RE THE SAME TWO CULPRITS RESPONSIBLE FOR STIFLING CREATIVITY IN BUSINESS RIGHT NOW: FEAR AND INERTIA.

HOW MASTERING TIME MANAGEMENT CAN HELP YOU SUCCEED

Time is an important factor in sparking individual creativity—since time, unlike money, is a resource that cannot be replaced. Time efficiency becomes part of the equation, especially if you are trying to meet a deadline.

You can manage your time better by planning out your day and reserving a certain number of minutes / hours on your project. Life can be full of distractions that slow projects down, but if you budget your time, it's possible to be much more productive.

Don't multitask; when you are developing ideas and in the creative process, stay focused. Remember, one of the strongest models and strategies for creativity is "The 3 I's": **Immersion, Incubation** and **Illumination**. Stay immersed and focused on the world your project / challenge lives in, setting aside enough time for each phase.

WHY YOU SHOULD COMMIT TO PERSONAL INSIGHTS AS CATALYSTS AND ANCHORS

BUILDING ON YOUR OWN EXPERIENCES

Use your own knowledge, experience, target insights and the creative / innovation brief (in a work setting) as an anchor from which more ideas can blossom. Stay close to your own passion and personality for the project unless you want to venture into something experimental.

Ask yourself what is the common thread that connects you personally with this project? And begin to develop new ideas from your own experiences. How can these basic ideas be combined to inspire an entirely new idea? Choose a theme that resonates with you personally so that you can build from a core of insights with which you are already familiar.

CREATIVITY CAN BE TAUGHT—AND LEARNED.

WHY THE MOTTO "DON'T STOP BELIEVIN'" NEVER FAILS

Know what the most important part of any successful innovative venture is?

Your mindset. Your belief.

Your absolute buy-in to the idea that yes, there is a different way—and yes, you will find it or you will invent it yourself, come hell or high water.

STORM STARTER EXERCISE 19: DISCOVERING YOUR CREATIVE SELF

How would you rate the individual "flow of creativity" (ability to be a fast idea generator) you observe presently in your own internal *Creative Storms*?

- ❏ NO FLOW
- ❏ LIMITED FLOW
- ❏ GOOD FLOW
- ❏ ADVANCED FLOW
- ❏ CREATIVE STORM FLOW

Why is that?

_____

_____

How could you turn that around?

_____

_____

What's stopping you?

_____

_____

CREATIVE STORM SUCCESS STORY: SPARKING IMAGINATION WITH PAUL SAN MARCO AND BROADWAY'S CHORUS LINE

When I performed the leading role of Paul San Marco in a stage production of *Chorus Line*, I embraced a creative process that unleashed my own internal *Creative Storm*. As introduced in PERFORMANCE Force 8, EMPOWER GENERATORS, I activated and followed "The Three I's": **Immersion, Incubation** and **Illumination.**

I needed to "immerse myself" in this role and get a better sense of what this Paul San Marco character—an actor trying to make it on Broadway—was all about and going through. It would help in my creating an innovative performance.

This character, Paul San Marco from Spanish Harlem, New York, was shy and introverted. In the show, Zach, the director, calls Paul on stage, and he emotionally relives his childhood and his very strained relationship with his parents.

During my "Immersion" and "Incubation" phase, I realized Paul and I had something in common: a very tough relationship with our mothers. So during every performance of this show, I would always conjure up my relationship with my mom and the emotional feelings I had about it. It helped me create an innovative performance that was insightful, relevant and memorable.

I unleashed my imaginative capacities by accessing my own emotional life and impulses and deepening my intuition. I used "Immersion" to help me broaden my imaginative responses and deepen emotional accessibility. My performance received standing ovations and earned awards, including being nominated for a *Best Supporting Actor Award*, at the ACT-CO FESTIVAL and winning the *Best Actor In A Leading Role* Award at Music Theatre Mississauga's Annual Gala.

STORM STARTER ACTION STEPS: FORCE 9, SPARK IMAGINATION

1. Accept that it is NOT only about your team's creativity BUT about YOUR own creativity as well, so keep your hands dirty by engaging with your team in the creative process, and have access to creative techniques you find effective to activate your own individual creativity.

2. Believe that creativity can be taught and learned, so be engaged and proactive in developing your own creativity and work to improve it often.

3. Become a master of time management.

4. Discipline yourself at switching from right brain to left brain (become seasoned at bringing together your intuition and logical thinking) so you can select the best ideas "strategically" and drive them into action.

PART III

KICK-STARTING YOUR CREATIVE STORM: SUMMARY AND NEXT STEPS

DURING THE CREATIVE STORM, THE 9 FORCES EXPECTEDLY COLLIDE IN A PERFECT STORM TO PRODUCE THE GREATEST, FIERCEST LEVELS OF PERFORMANCE AND INNOVATION YOUR COMPANY HAS EVER SEEN.

THE CREATIVE STORM UNLEASHED: UNITING THE 9 FORCES

FINAL THOUGHTS FOR IGNITING CREATIVE LEADERSHIP AND MANAGING CREATIVITY IN YOUR ORGANIZATION

Although you have reached the end of the book, you are only beginning your *Creative Storm* journey. **The 9 Forces** in this book (summarized on the next page) will help you lead your people as a Triple Threat Creative Leader, build a *Creative Storming Culture* and push yourself and your employees to achieve *Creative Storm*-level performance, thus ushering in a new age of astonishing innovation, engagement, profitability and growth for your business.

I end this book with my two final **Storm Starter Exercises** and my **Creative Leadership Self-Assessment Quiz**— to serve as the ultimate test of your Creative Leadership and ability to unleash *The Creative Storm*.

THE NEW ROLE OF THE LEADER: UNLEASH THE 9 FORCES OF CREATIVE LEADERSHIP

F1	**C**HAMPION COMMUNICATION	LEADERSHIP
F2	**R**ELEASE CHEERLEADER	LEADERSHIP
F3	**EL**EVATE STRATEGY	LEADERSHIP
F4	**A**CTIVATE CLIMATES	CULTURE
F5	**T**RIGGER COLLABORATION	CULTURE
F6	**I**NSPIRE RISK	CULTURE
F7	**V**ALUE EMPATHY	PERFORMANCE
F8	**EM**POWER GENERATORS	PERFORMANCE
F9	**S**PARK IMAGINATION	PERFORMANCE

THE ULTIMATE GOAL AND ROLE OF THE LEADER IS TO:

1. Produce **CREATIVES:** easy collaborators and fast idea generators who are productive as hell and frighteningly efficient, and

2. Unleash a **CREATIVE S**(TORM)

STORM STARTER EXERCISE 20: THE FORCES AWAKEN AUDIT

The Force I'm using and applying most consistently is:

_____

_____

_____

_____

_____

The Force I use every once in a while, but plan to further awaken and stir up is:

_____

_____

_____

_____

_____

The Force I rarely use but am most excited to kick-start and act on immediately is:

_____

_____

_____

_____

_____

STORM STARTER EXERCISE 21: THE CREATIVE STORM UNLEASHED

How often do people from your company share new ideas with you? Do you have time for it? Are you open to it?

_____

_____

_____

_____

What do you do when someone from your company shares a new idea with you?

_____

_____

_____

_____

What do you do to encourage employees to share their ideas? Do you know how to bring those ideas out?

_____

_____

_____

_____

_____

Do you make time for your team when they are in the first stages of the creative process?

_____

_____

_____

_____

_____

How do you presently reward the innovative activities of your employees?

_____

_____

_____

_____

Are you open to taking a risk using ideas other than your own?

_____

_____

_____

_____

Are you open to unlearn and forget past processes, ideas and success formulas?

_____

_____

_____

_____

What are 3 things you can do starting today to instill a more collaborative culture of innovation?

1. _____
_____
2. _____
_____
3. _____
_____

Write down 3-4 stories that represent how you dealt with other people's ideas, good or bad.

_____
_____
_____
_____
_____
_____
_____

Share these stories at your next meeting; then ask people to write their own experiences about collaboration to add to the mix.

Storm Starter Bonus Exercise: For one week, every day, each employee on your team needs to bring you one idea. Something new, that brings about a "change" in process, culture or content.

WHEN THOSE THREE WEATHER CELLS COLLIDED IN THE ATLANTIC OCEAN IN 1991 TO FORM "THE PERFECT STORM," AN UNSTOPPABLE MONSTER OF A SUPER-STORM WAS CREATED AND UNLEASHED.

THE CREATIVE LEADERSHIP TRIFECTA FORMULA:

CREATIVE LEADERSHIP
+ CREATIVE CULTURE
+ CREATIVE PERFORMANCE
= THE CREATIVE STORM

Creative leadership, a creative culture and creative individuals interacting and reinforcing each other in a continuous dynamic system results in *The Creative Storm*.

CREATIVE LEADERSHIP SELF-ASSESSMENT QUIZ

Based on a typical day, rate yourself against the following statements by circling one of the numbers:

1 = NEVER   2 = RARELY   3 = SOMETIMES   4 = OFTEN   5 = ALWAYS

CHAMPION COMMUNICATION - LEADERSHIP

I give everyone an equal voice and push people to really listen to each other.

1   2   3   4   5

I discuss ideas with employees and my team in person.

1   2   3   4   5

I communicate my direction and vision effectively, and provide helpful guidance and feedback.

1   2   3   4   5

I know how to advocate for ideas (even those I dislike, but realize they offer value to the organization), persuading others of their value, and present my case without steam-rolling those who object.

1   2   3   4   5

RELEASE CHEERLEADER - LEADERSHIP

I establish trust, honesty and belief by giving away credit.

    1   2   3   4   5

I am persistent with my positivity, radiating optimistic, contagious energy, so that I can keep people enthusiastic and inspire them to do even better.

    1   2   3   4   5

I routinely use strategies to keep my team's energy fired up so they never lose their mojo.

    1   2   3   4   5

I give my employees and teams more than five positive comments for every criticism, challenging ourselves to identify positive aspects to even the craziest of ideas.

    1   2   3   4   5

ELEVATE STRATEGY - LEADERSHIP

I am seasoned at candor, brutal honesty and decisiveness, and know when to—and am able to—speak the tough truth.

    1   2   3   4   5

I encourage others to make decisions but defy them when I must, being flexible but defiant, and knowing how and when to rein people in.

    1   2   3   4   5

I am constantly in a balancing act between my intellect (brain), intuition (gut), and team—then making a decision based on that.

1   2   3   4   5

With a strong sense of authority and the courage to make tough decisions, I am ready and willing to kill ideas I love, making unpopular decisions for the sake of the work and business objectives.

1   2   3   4   5

ACTIVATE CLIMATES - CULTURE

I create a culture where everyone can have ideas and feel that they're valued, celebrating both success and failure.

1   2   3   4   5

I know how to recognize and blow away the "TOP 6" biggest barriers to creativity in business—and ensure they don't reassert themselves. I protect my teams from hostile environments and clear paths for them around obstacles.

1   2   3   4   5

I don't hover, judge or criticize while my teams are working, because that leads to underperformance and underthinking. I can recognize when I, or other managers and leaders, are creativity killers.

1   2   3   4   5

I ignite a culture of curiosity, keep on inquiring, keep on probing, keep on learning.

1   2   3   4   5

TRIGGER COLLABORATION - CULTURE

I am committed to replacing "idea ownership" with "idea improvement"—grabbing ideas, developing them further, then handing them back.

1   2   3   4   5

I accept that I don't have to be the one to come up with all the ideas, knowing how and when to stop clinging obsessively to one idea—namely, my own.

1   2   3   4   5

I foster an environment where innovation and new ideas are not only safe, but encouraged and expected—creating structures, time, and spaces where ideas can be discussed and collaboration can flow. I give everyone, regardless of their position, the opportunity to be heard.

1   2   3   4   5

I co-create future products, services and processes with employees, customers and external partners, staying open to engaging those willing to play in a "test lab" environment.

1   2   3   4   5

INSPIRE RISK - CULTURE

I often push myself, my team and my clients out of our / their comfort zones to challenge assumptions and disrupt the status quo, constantly forcing ourselves to consider ideas we wouldn't have previously considered.

1   2   3   4   5

I encourage my team to use established conventions as the starting point to drive innovation and change.

1   2   3   4   5

I often employ "creative destruction." To achieve new success, I will kill old processes, unlearning and selectively forgetting past success formulas, no matter how effective previously.

1   2   3   4   5

I know how to experiment and test ideas in a safe way, without damaging my brand, starting with small projects and small budgets, then test, learn and prove.

1   2   3   4   5

VALUE EMPATHY - PERFORMANCE

I encourage myself and my team to use market research and data, staying informed about new markets and emerging technologies, and following blogs, trendspotters and websites reporting on our product or content's industry—because it's the soil where ideas grow.

1   2   3   4   5

I proactively put myself and my teams in our customer's shoes, staying open to allowing myself and my team to get out of the office and hang out where our customer does.

1   2   3   4   5

I know how to leverage empathy to enhance decision-making, defend the big idea and support and fuel creativity.

    1   2   3   4   5

I am open to dialogue and discussion in the marketplace, fostering open innovation and listening to the wisdom of my customers.

    1   2   3   4   5

EMPOWER GENERATORS - PERFORMANCE

I have an unlimited arsenal of creative techniques and processes and volunteer and inject them into my employees and teams regularly, suggesting—but not necessarily imposing—a process.

    1   2   3   4   5

I encourage turning minds off to turn creativity on.

    1   2   3   4   5

I embrace a melting pot attitude: recognizing and capitalizing on skills and traits of employees and accommodating to their strengths, believing that diversity in all its shapes, colors and flavors helps build creative cultures.

    1   2   3   4   5

I magnify the creativity in everyone I come into contact with, making retention and talent development a conscious choice.

    1   2   3   4   5

SPARK IMAGINATION - PERFORMANCE

I understand that it is all about my team's creativity AND my own creativity as well, so I keep my hands dirty by engaging with my team in the creative process, and have creative techniques that I access and use to activate my own individual creativity.

     1   2   3   4   5

I believe that creativity can be taught and learned, so I am engaged in developing my own creativity and work regularly to improve that creativity.

     1   2   3   4   5

I am a master of time management.

     1   2   3   4   5

I am disciplined at switching from right brain to left brain (seasoned at bringing together my intuition and logical thinking) so I can select the best ideas "strategically" and drive them into action.

     1   2   3   4   5

OVERALL SCORE (Total each column and then get the sum of those 5 totals.) _____

As you review your scores for each of the nine sections, here are some questions to consider:

HIGH SCORES (you rated yourself between 150 and 180): Look at the high scores you gave yourself. Why did you rate yourself high in those areas? What is the process or habit that supports that score?

Often you can perform at a high level in some aspect of Creative Leadership and not be aware that what you are doing is unique.

Record at least one process or habit you are doing well that resulted in your high score.

_____

_____

MID-RANGE SCORES (you rated yourself between 125 and 150): Look for areas where you excel and have good performance. How can you reinforce these to ensure that they continue to happen?

Look at areas that you rated a 1, 2, or 3—what is the pattern that is keeping you from scoring higher?

Record at least one habit you have that resulted in the low score.

_____

_____

LOW SCORES (you rated yourself below 125): What are you doing that is inhibiting your Creative Leadership performance? Think about your habits, innovation strategies, leadership philosophies and management approaches that you presently use to inspire and lead innovation. By becoming more aware of your patterns, you will be more able to create the change you need.

List 3 of the most obvious areas in need of improvement on the next page (here are some examples):

➤ *I don't have the creative techniques I need to support and boost my team.*

➤ *I am a "Negative Nelly" and usually kill ideas too quickly.*

➤ *I don't take my responsibilities to be inspiring and passionate seriously.*

➤ *I'm not a very good presenter of ideas.*

➤ *There's too much inertia in my team and organization, but I don't know how to get us unstuck.*

➤ *I often hover, judge and criticize while my teams are working.*

I want to change / improve

_____

_____

_____

_____

I want to change / improve

_____

_____

_____

_____

I want to change / improve

_____

_____

_____

_____

Keep these areas of development in mind. The more focused you are on what you want to change, the more likely you are to navigate change effectively and unleash new levels of creativity, innovation and profitability—so you can take your industry by storm.

FINAL THOUGHTS

THE MOST POWERFUL FORCE IN BUSINESS AND IN LIFE IS CREATIVITY

ABOUT NELSON CABRAL

Creatively acclaimed and internationally recognized, Creative Leadership & Innovation Expert Nelson Cabral has spent his career using creativity to build business. He's been leading teams, building companies and inspiring breakthrough innovative thinking within Fortune 500 brands for over 25 years.

As the world's only *Triple Threat Creative Leadership Expert* and management consultant to brands and CEOs, he shares with audiences his management approaches and leadership philosophies from decades worth of experiences as a Triple Threat Creative Leader: award-winning Advertising Executive Creative Director, TV Director and Broadway Musical Theatre Leading Man.

He's an award-winning advertising Writer and Creative Director for some of the world's most respected global brands including adidas, Air Canada, Anheuser-Busch, Bridgestone-Firestone, Cadbury, GE, Kellogg's, Microsoft, Procter & Gamble, Toshiba and many others.

His world-class, breakthrough ideas and superior levels of creativity and innovation have been recognized by The Cannes Lions International Festival of Creativity, The

London International Advertising Awards, The New York Festivals of Advertising, The Crystals, The Mobius Awards, The Marketing Awards, and his Pro-Line "Bar Hopping Aliens" TV spot won first place, "Best TV Spot in Canada", in Playback Magazine's TOP SPOT AWARDS.

Nelson's directed celebrities, Grammy award-winning music icons and international artists around the world, producing innovative content people talk about and love. He's also performed some of musical theatre's most sought-after leading man roles, garnering standing ovations and awards for his innovative portrayals—including The Emcee in *Cabaret*, Jesus in *Godspell* and Pierrepont Finch in *How To Succeed In Business Without Really Trying*.

Now a Professional Speaker, Corporate Trainer, Leadership Consultant and Innovation Facilitator, Nelson and his boutique training firm *CABRAL Creative Leadership International* continues to energize leaders, teams and organizations to boost management effectiveness, drive superior levels of performance and build pervasive cultures of innovation. Today, Nelson travels, speaks, writes, engages and shares as generously in person as he does in this game-changing book.

BOOK NELSON CABRAL TO SPEAK AT YOUR NEXT MEETING OR EVENT

As the world's only *Triple Threat Creative Leadership Expert* and a top-rated Keynote Speaker, Nelson delivers inspiring and actionable keynotes on innovation, creativity and leadership.

"I was at a leadership conference where the Keynote Speaker was **Nelson Cabral** who made a really great presentation on innovation and Creative Leadership. The perspective that caught my attention was that while many speak to what innovation is, and how to innovate, he spoke to **The 9 Forces of Creative Leadership** that can help leaders to **unleash *The Creative Storm*** in their organization. Nelson's experience and extremely engaging personality, as well as his passion for helping leaders to help themselves, would, in my opinion, help any organization get enthused and excited about innovation and creativity. I would strongly recommend that you consider him as a suitable speaker at any event or executive learning opportunity."

SHERIN V EMMANUEL MIS, PMP
CANADA REVENUE AGENCY

THE CREATIVE STORM: UNLEASHING THE 9 FORCES OF CREATIVE LEADERSHIP

Nelson conducts his flagship keynote presentation and training seminar for groups of senior executives and business leaders who want HIGHER performing teams, MORE innovation, BETTER leadership and STRONGER culture and engagement.

The Creative Storm explains how to get creative juices flowing, how to innovate to stay ahead, and prepare you for the disruptive forces at work so you can take your industry by storm.

Depending on your format, time available and meeting objectives, Nelson's presentation can run from thirty minutes to three days. It zeroes in on the core issues which Creative Leaders face on a daily basis . . . managing, inspiring and organizing more collaborative, creative and successful teams.

For availability and booking information, call your favorite Speakers Bureau or you can reach Nelson directly at (506) 536-7004.

RESOURCES FOR BUILDING CREATIVE LEADERSHIP

www.NelsonCabral.ca

CABRAL Creative Leadership International offers a complete range of learning tools, training and coaching services to help you turn around lagging leadership with strong Creative Leadership skills to navigate today's fast-paced and ever-shifting business universe. Restoring lost creative mojos back in line with the high performance creative culture your organization deserves is our mission.

If you want relief from slow idea generators, hard collaborators, and ineffective team relationships, visit our content-rich website. There you will find Nelson's blog, nelsoncabralTV, free podcasts and audio learning programs to keep you inspired and at your highest level, *The Creative Storm Report* (free monthly newsletter) as well as Nelson's other books. Get engaged to begin replacing traditional employer / employee relationships with cutting-edge approaches to developing the best and brightest talent.

It's also a great place for tools, Cheat Sheets, Worksheets and products for Senior Executives, high potentials, team leaders and managers who want to lead and inspire teams to higher levels of creativity, innovation and profitability.

Get your complete set of downloadable worksheets, bonuses and companion tools by visiting www.nelsoncabral.ca/resources

SPEND A WEEKEND WITH NELSON CABRAL: THE CREATIVE STORM FORCES AWAKEN WEEKEND

Once a year, creative leaders from around the world come together for one of the most powerful personal and professional development workshops they will ever attend. The Creative Storm FORCES AWAKEN Weekend (CSFA) is a life-changing experience that will help you discover a transformational process to manage creativity for the highest levels of innovation. CSFA takes place in a "most creative" city every year, like London, New York, San Francisco, Montreal, Berlin, Lisbon, Paris or Toronto (and is one of the most inspiring learning experiences you will ever have). For more details and to register for the next CSFA Weekend, visit nelsoncabral.ca today.

FINAL THOUGHTS

IT TAKES A VILLAGE. Thank you to all my friends, my family, my clients, my book team (special mention to David Newman, Christopher Murray and Peter Chapman), the Creative Leaders, creative partners and collaborators who have inspired me through the years (special mention to Gary McGuire, Jeffrey R. Fish, Bryson Gilbert, Frank Streicher, Nathalie Gallant, Martin Shewchuk, Gary Hesketh, Bill Keenan, Peter Lanyon, Jeff Durocher, Tony Nicol, Megan Fullerton, Michael McCabe, Miguel Leblanc, Maurice Belliveau, Lisa Paschal, Jocelyne Saulnier, James Wheldon, Lianne Dizon, Bob Goulart, John Gallo and Michael Caccamo) and my colleagues in the Canadian Association of Professional Speakers, National Speakers Association, Global Speakers Federation and The Alliance of Canadian Cinema, Television and Radio Artists. Your faith in me and support of my work has surpassed my wildest dreams.

Share *The Creative Storm* with your friends, family members and colleagues. Buy 50 copies and receive a 50% discount off the retail price. Call (506) 536-7004 for special pricing on larger quantities.

Send us your comments. We'd like to hear your success stories, insights and any ideas you have for our future reference and additional books and programs.

NELSON CABRAL

PRESIDENT & CHIEF CREATIVE OFFICER

CABRAL Creative Leadership International Inc.
Email: nelson@nelsoncabral.ca
Call: (506) 536-7004
Visit: www.nelsoncabral.ca
Connect: www.linkedin.com/in/cabralcreative

NELSON CABRAL